TERROR'S

TERROR'S SOURCE
The Ideology of Wahhabi-Salafism and its Consequences

VINCENZO OLIVETI

AMADEUSBOOKS

Published by

AMADEUS BOOKS

P.O. BOX 10743
BIRMINGHAM B12 8ZX
UNITED KINGDOM

ISBN 0-9543729-0-5 *paperback*

Printed in the United Arab Emirates

This book *identifies* the ideological source of terrorism emanating from the Islamic World; *differentiates* between it and traditional 'orthodox' Islam; *examines* in detail all its tenets and doctrines; *explains* how it has spread and how it is gaining ground; *warns* of the dangers of its continued growth; and, finally, *prescribes* how to combat and defeat this ideology and thereby stop terrorism at its source.

CONTENTS

Horror and Shock on September 11th, 2001

THE HORROR

THE WORLD was horrified and astounded on September 11th, 2001 when four commercial airplanes were hijacked in mid-air by suicidal terrorists over the skies of the United States, and two of these planes were crashed into the Twin Towers in New York city (bringing them hurtling to the ground and killing around 3,000 people in the process),[1] one was crashed into the Pentagon (killing around 200 people) in Washington DC, and the fourth one was crashed into the ground in Pennsylvania whilst also on its way to Washington. Everyone aboard all four planes was also killed including the hijackers themselves who turned out to be only nineteen in number on all four planes.

THE SHOCK

The whole world was profoundly shocked and aghast by these events. Five factors in particular combined to accentuate[2] this

---

[1] The official estimates of the number of victims of the tragedy keep changing (from 7,300 shortly after September 11th to around 2,800 six months later), perhaps partly because American prestige and morale are at stake, and partly because a huge compensation was created for the families of the victims. A final list of names of victims has yet to be published.

[2] In 1994 between 800,000 and 1,000,000 innocent Tutsi civilians were systematically hacked to death with machetes and axes by Hutu

reaction: (1) The sheer mercilessness and brutality of the attacks, as reflected in the number of innocent people killed indiscriminately, many of them being women, children, old people and even disabled people. (2) The spectacular nature of the events: these were not 3,000 people who died quietly in bed due to old age, but rather people who died in explosions, commotion, fire, steel and countless human dramas involving desperate rescue efforts and tales of heroism and individual sacrifice. (3) The CNN effect: CNN caught all the spectacular scenes and images on television — from the planes crashing into the Twin Towers; to people jumping to their death from these in order to escape being burnt alive; to the Towers collapsing; to the smoke and carnage afterwards; to the final conversations of the hijacked passengers; and, finally, to the emotions of the families and the survivors — and broadcast them instantaneously all over the world again and again for the next three weeks, reaching literally hundreds of millions of people. (4) The fact that these 'attacks' occurred against the very symbols of American financial and military power: America, as the world's only remaining real superpower, had hitherto enjoyed an aura of invincibility. (5) The fact that the indiscriminate slaughter of thousands of innocent civilians was committed by a group that claimed to act on behalf of Islam, one of history's greatest religions, and a faith to which one fifth of the world's belongs.

THE CONFUSION

How could all this happen? Why did it happen? Could it simply be said that the militants behind these events — namely,

---

Interahamwe gangs in the African country of Rwanda, over the space of 100 days. If the world community was shocked, it certainly did not show it, and at any rate no one did anything to stop them. By contrast the world *was* genuinely shocked by the events of September 11th, 2001.

Preface

Usama bin Laden and his terrorist network al-Qaʻeda (Bin Laden was also thought to be behind, among other terrorist attacks, the bombing of the USS *Cole* in Yemen in 2000 and the simultaneous bombings of the US embassies in Nairobi, Kenya and Darussalam, Tanzania in 1998) — no more represented Islam than Timothy McVeigh represented Christianity when on April 19th, 1995 he bombed Oklahoma City killing 168 people, or than did Hitler when he caused the death of tens of millions of people in the Second World War?

Or does the Islamic world really hate the USA? Why would it? Has the USA not been generally benevolent towards the Arab and Islamic worlds over the course of the twentieth century (with the notable exception of its unqualified support for Israel during the years 1960–2000)? Objectively speaking, is it not true that during the nineteenth century and the first half of the twentieth century the USA was never an *occupying* colonial power in the Islamic world (unlike Britain, France, Italy, Russia, Holland, and, to a lesser extent, Germany, Spain and Portugal), and that during the twentieth century the USA never unfairly divided up Islamic countries nor gave away their lands (unlike Britain and France)? Neither did it *ever* commit genocide and pogroms against Muslim populations, unlike European countries like France, Italy and Russia and, more recently, countries such as Serbia, Burma and Zanzibar (or rather, Tanzania). Nor, did the USA even merely suppress Muslim minorities and Islamic culture (like India and China). In the years 1980–2000 has it not been the first to take concrete action to defend Muslims in places such as Afghanistan, Bosnia, Albania, Kosovo, Somalia, Chechnya and Kuwait? Do Muslims not love to migrate to the USA and live there? Also, did not the USA's leadership — and in particular the White House — in the late 1990s and in the New Millennium (up until September 11th and indeed since) go out of its way to respectfully and warmly recognize the religion of Islam, and the positive contributions of the millions of Americans Muslims to the USA's social and moral life? Does all this count for nothing in Muslim eyes?

Finally, and perhaps most confusing of all, *did not the Prophet Muhammad explicitly ban and condemn the killing of civilians, women and children etc., under any circumstances*? After all, as most adult Muslims know, the Caliph Abu Bakr (the immediate successor to the Prophet) summarized, in practically his first act as Caliph, the Prophet's owns laws of *Jihad* (Islamic Holy War, in legitimate self-defense) to the Muslim army as follows:

> *Do not betray; do not carry grudges; do not deceive; do not mutilate; do not kill children; do not kill the elderly; do not kill women. Do not destroy beehives or burn them; do not cut down fruit-bearing trees; do not slaughter sheep, cattle or camels, except for food. You will come upon people who spend their lives in monasteries (i.e. Christian monks), leave them to what they have dedicated their lives ... Push forward in the Name of God.* [3]

In what follows we will endeavour to answer all these questions by examining the ideology that implacably rails against USA without discernment and without an eye to history; the ideology that permits, nay, encourages, the killing of innocent civilians, despite traditional Islam's strict ban against this; the ideology that *turns its back on over one thousand years of Islam, in the name of Islam*; the ideology of radical *Salafism*.

[3] KhairAllah Tulfah, *Abu Bakr*, vol.12, p.36 (translated by the author).

I

The House of Islam

W HAT IS ISLAM? The rest of the world is confused. To the non-Muslim the subject is profoundly alien and complicated. And terrorism and prejudice have combined to misrepresent it on the popular level in the West. In what follows we try to give a basic synopsis of the religion, because without this synopsis it is impossible to understand anything about its nature and behaviour.

THE RELIGION OF ISLAM

The religion of Islam is based on belief in the One God (who in Arabic is called *Allah*). It was founded by the Prophet Muhammad (570–632 CE) in the ancient cities of Mecca and Medina, in the West Coast of the Arabian Peninsula (known as the *Hijaz*). God Revealed to the Prophet Muhammad the Holy Qur'an, the Sacred Book of Islam. The religion this created, however, was not a new message but simply a final and total Arabic restatement of God's messages to the Hebrew Prophets and to Jesus. The Holy Qur'an says:

> *Say ye: we believe in God and that which is revealed unto us and that which was revealed unto Abraham, and Ishmael, and Isaac, and Jacob, and the Tribes, and that which Moses and Jesus received, and that which the Prophets received from their Lord. We make no distinction between any of them, and unto Him we have submitted.* (The Holy Qur'an, 2:136)

I

Moreover, the Holy Qur'an did not even exclude the possibility of revelations other than those that were given to the Prophets mentioned in the Bible (and thus did not exclude the possibility of other genuine ancient religions other than Judaism, Christianity and Islam). God says, in the Holy Qur'an:

Verily We have sent Messengers before thee [O Muhammad]. About some of them have We told thee, and about some have we not told thee... (40:78)

And verily We have raised in every nation a Messenger [proclaiming]: serve God and shun false gods... (16:36).

THE ESSENCE OF ISLAM

The essence and substance of Islam can be easily summed up by three major principles (which are also successive stages in the spiritual life): *Islam* (meaning 'submission to God's will'); *Iman* (meaning 'faith in God'), and *Ihsan* (meaning 'virtue through constant regard to, and awareness of, God'). The second Caliph, the great 'Umar ibn al-Khattab, related that:

One day when we were sitting [in Medina] with the Messenger of God [the Prophet Muhammad] there came unto us a man whose clothes were of exceeding whiteness and whose hair was of exceeding blackness, nor were there any signs of travel upon him, although none of us knew him. He sat down knee upon knee opposite the Prophet, upon whose thighs he placed the palms of his hands, saying: 'O Muhammad, tell me what is the surrender (Islam)'. The Messenger of God answered him saying: 'The surrender is to testify that there is no god but God and that Muhammad is God's Messenger, to perform the prayer, bestow the alms, fast Ramadan and make if thou canst, the pilgrimage to the Holy House.' He said: 'Thou hast spoken

2

truly,' and we were amazed that having questioned him he should corroborate him. Then he said: 'Tell me what is faith (Iman)'. He answered: 'To believe in God and His Angels and his Books and His Messengers and the Last Day [the Day of Judgement], and to believe that no good or evil cometh but by His Providence.' 'Thou hast spoken truly,' he said, and then: 'Tell me what is excellence (Ihsan).' He answered: 'To worship God as if thou sawest Him, for if Thou seest Him not, yet seeth He thee.' 'Thou hast spoken truly,' he said ... Then the stranger went away, and I stayed a while after he had gone; and the Prophet said to me: 'O 'Umar, knowest thou the questioner, who he was?' I said: 'God and His Messenger know best.' He said: 'It was Gabriel [the Archangel]. He came unto you to teach you your religion.' [4]

Thus *Islam* as such consists of 'five pillars': (1) the *Shahada-tayn* or the 'testimony of faith' (whose inward meaning is the acknowledgement of God). (2) The five daily prayers (whose inward meaning is the attachment to God). (3) Giving alms or *Zakat* — one-fortieth of one's income and savings annually to the poor and destitute (whose inward meaning is the detachment from the world). (4) Fasting the Holy month of *Ramadan* annually (whose inward meaning is detachment from the body and from the ego). (5) Making the *Hajj* (whose inner meaning is to return to one's true inner heart, the mysterious square, black-shrouded Ka'ba in Mecca being the outward symbol of this heart).

Thus also *Iman* as such consists of belief in all the essential doctrines of religion (and the inner meaning of this is that one should not go through the motions of religion and of the five

---

[4] *Sahih Muslim*, 'Kitab al-Iman', 1, n.1. (The *Hadiths* of the Prophet, like all sacred texts, are written above in italics.)

pillars of Islam blindly or robotically, but rather have real faith and certainty in one's heart).

Thus, finally, *Ihsan* as such consists of believing that God always sees us, and therefore that one must be virtuous and sincere in all one's actions. In this connection the Prophet said: *'By Him in whose Hand is my Life, none of you believes till he loves for his neighbour what he loves for himself'*.[5] In summary, we could say that the essence of Islam is exactly the Two Commandments upon which Jesus said hangs *all the Law and the Prophets:*

> *And Jesus answered him, The first of all commandments is...*
> *the Lord our God is one Lord; And thou shalt love the Lord*
> *thy God with all thy heart, and with all thy soul, and with*
> *all thy understanding, and with all thy strength: this is the*
> *first commandment. And the second commandment is like,*
> *namely this, Thou shalt love thy neighbour as thyself. There is*
> *none other commandment greater than these.*[6]

THE CANON OF ISLAM

Islam does not, like Christianity, have a clergy. There is no temporal or even spiritual institute that holds it together or unifies it. So how did it hold together — and indeed, flourish — for the last fourteen centuries approximately, when its scholars and temporal policy-makers keep changing and dying out over time? How did it remain so homogeneous that the Islam of 1900 AD was doctrinally exactly the same as the Islam of 700 AD? Where did its internal checks and balances come from?

---

[5] *Sahih Muslim*, 'Kitab al-Iman', 18, n.72.
[6] *The Gospel according to Mark* 12:29–31, (See also Deuteronomy 6:5; and Matthew 22:37–40).

The House of Islam

The answer is that Islam has a traditional canon:[7] a collection of sacred texts which everyone has agreed are authoritative and definitive, and which 'fix' the *principles* of belief, practice, law, theology and doctrine throughout the ages. All that Muslim scholars (called *sheikh*s or *imam*s) have left to do is to interpret these texts and work out their practical applications and details (and the principles of interpretation and elaboration are themselves 'fixed' by these texts), so that in Islam a person is only considered learned to the extent that he can demonstrate his knowledge of these texts. This does not mean that Islam is a religion of limitations for these texts are a vast ocean and their principles can be inwardly worked out almost infinitely in practice. It does mean, however, that Islam is 'fixed' and has certain limits beyond which it will not go. This *is an extremely important concept to understand*, because misunderstanding it, and setting aside the traditional canon of Islam, leads to people killing and assassinating others in the name of religion, as we shall see. The traditional canon of Islam is what protects not just the religion of Islam itself, but the world (including Muslims themselves) from terrorism, murder and oppression in the name of Islam. The canon is Islam's internal check and balance system; it is what safeguards its moderation; it is 'self-censorship' and its ultimate safety feature.

To be more specific, the traditional Sunni Islamic Canon starts with the Qur'an itself; then the great traditional Commentaries upon it (e.g. Tabari; Razi; Zamakhshari/Baydawi; Qurtubi; Jalalayn; Ibn Kathir; Shawkani; and al-Wahidi's *Asbab al-Nuzul*); then the eight traditional collections of *Hadith,* the sayings of the Prophet, (e.g. Muslim; Bukhari; Tirmidhi; Ibn Hanbal; al-Nasa'i; al-Sijistani; al-Darimi and Ibn Maja); the

---

[7] Even the English word 'canon' comes from the Arabic word *kanun* meaning 'law' or 'principle'.

5

later *Muhaddithin,* or Traditionists (e.g. Bayhaqi; Baghawi; Nawawi, and 'Asqalani); then the traditional biographical and historical works of *Sira* (Ibn Ishaq, Ibn Sa'd; Waqidi; Azraqi; Tabari; and Suhayli); the *Risala* of al-Shafi'i; the *Muwatta'* of Imam Malik; the *Ihya' 'Ulum al-Din* of Ghazali; Ash'arite and Maturidian theology; the (original) *'Aqida* of Tahawi; Imam Jazuli's *Dala'il al-Khayrat,* and finally — albeit only extrinsically — *Jahiliyya* poetry (as a background reference for the semantic connotations of words in the Arabic language). We give a specific (but not exhaustive) list here in order to minimize the possibility of misunderstanding.

ISLAM IN HISTORY

It is evidently not possible to do justice to the role of Islam in world history, thought and civilization in a few words, but the following paragraph by Britain's Prince Charles attempts it:

> The mediaeval Islamic world, from Central Asia to the shores of the Atlantic, was a world where scholars and men of learning flourished. But because we have tended to see Islam as the enemy, as an alien culture, society, and system of belief, we have tended to ignore or erase its great relevance to our own history. For example, we have under-estimated the importance of eight hundred years of Islamic society and culture in Spain between the 8th and 15th centuries. The contribution of Muslim Spain to the preservation of classical learning during the Dark Ages, and to the first flowerings of the Renaissance, has long been recognized. But Islamic Spain was much more then a mere larder where Hellenistic knowledge was kept for later consumption by the emerging modern Western world. Not only did Muslim Spain gather and preserve the intellectual content

of ancient Greek and Roman civilization, it also interpreted and expanded upon that civilization, and made a vital contribution of its own in so many fields of human endeavour — in science, astronomy, mathematics, algebra (itself an Arabic word), law, history, medicine, pharmacology, optics, agriculture, architecture, theology, music. Averroes [Ibn Rushd] and Avenzoor [Ibn Zuhr], like their counterparts Avicenna [Ibn Sina] and Rhazes [Abu Bakr al-Razi] in the East, contributed to the study and practice of medicine in ways from which Europe benefited for centuries afterwards.[8]

ISLAM TODAY

Today it is estimated that over one fifth of the world's population of over 6 billion people (that is, more than 1.2 billion people), are Muslims. They live mostly in a huge belt around the centre of the globe comprising basically the northern part of Africa (there are over 400 million Muslims in Africa) and the southern part of Asia (there are at least 750 million Muslims in Asia). Thus the international OIC (Organization of the Islamic Conference) comprises of 56 states where Muslims are a majority, out of a total of around 189 member states of the United Nations. There are also up to 50 million Muslims living as (mostly immigrant) minorities in Europe and the Americas, including up to 7 million Muslims in the USA.

Furthermore, although Islam is on paper only the second-largest religion in the world after Christianity, the religion of Islam is generally far more pervasive in the daily lives of Muslims than Christianity is in the lives of Christians: indeed, the total

---

[8] H. R. H. The Prince of Wales, 'Islam and the West', a lecture given at the Sheldonian Theatre, Oxford on October 27th, 1993, pp.17–18.

number of worshippers in mosques on Fridays (the Muslim holy day) far exceeds that of Christians on Sundays (the Christian day of rest). The majority of Muslims pray ritually five times a day, whereas the majority of Christians formally pray on average only once a week. Also, Islam is the fastest growing religion in the world, whereas the Christian faith is being everywhere corroded either by New Age 'spiritualisms' or by atheism, agnosticism and secularism.

Despite all these signs of apparent 'spiritual vigour', however, Islam remains today technologically, politically, economically, militarily the weakest[9] of the world's major civilizations (with the notable exception of the 'African civilization'):[10]

(1) **Technologically**, it suffices to note that not one major technological invention or scientific breakthrough in the whole twentieth century — the century of invention, the century which saw more invention and technological change than the rest of history combined — originates from Islamic countries.

(2) **Politically**, we note that 75 per cent of the world's refugees are Muslims, and that no Muslim country has a permanent

---

[9] It is worth remembering that for one thousand years, from 700–1700 CE, Islam was more or less the world's dominant civilization in these respects, and that the Ottomans had been at the gates of Vienna as late as 1683, and had even conquered the Ukraine ten years prior to that.

[10] The concept of distinct 'major civilizations' of the world was crystallized by Professor Samuel P. Huntington of Harvard University, in his seminal and now world-famous article 'The Clash of Civilizations' in the Summer 1993 edition of *Foreign Affairs*. Specifically, he identified these as Confucian/Chinese; Japanese/Buddhist; Hindu; Islamic; African; Western; Slavic-Orthodox; Latin-American. In light of their religious common origin and their increasing political and cultural solidarity, however, we would ourselves merge these last three as Western/Christian, and also add Jewish to the list as a distinct civilization.

seat on the United Nations Security Council, whereas Britain and France, countries of only approximately 60 million people each, do.

(3) **Economically**, we note that with the exception of small oil-rich Arab countries (whose wealth anyway has relatively little 'trickle-down'), the 'Islamic civilization' is also on average the poorest in the world (next to the African), and that the average growth rate in Islamic countries is significantly smaller than that of India or China. Even with Arab oil money the total GDP of Islamic countries is only 2 per cent of the world's 'total GDP', that is, only 10 per cent of what it should be according to the size of its population.

(4) **Militarily**, we note that for all the images of Muslims toting kalashnikovs in the Western media, there is not a single war in the twentieth century that Muslims have won over non-Muslims when unaided by the West, and even the struggles for liberation which led to freedom from colonial occupation (as in Algeria in the 1960s, for example) were never won on the battle-field. Moreover, indigenous Muslim populations are militarily still oppressed — and their aspirations suppressed — practically wherever they naturally come into contact with or border non-Muslim indigenous populations: from the Christian West African states to the Philippines, from Palestine to China (particularly in the Xinjiang province), from Kosovo and Bosnia (where, in the early 1990s, 300,000 Muslims were murdered by Serbs in concentration camps and in their own villages, and 100,000 Muslim women were raped as a 'weapon of war') to Kashmir and India (it is not insignificant that Muslims are the poorest and least educated of all Indians, and Christians the richest and best educated); and from Chechnya and Nagorno-Karabach to Burma. In fact, the only place Muslims have been

able to hold their own (or even are the oppressors) is on the demarcation with (non-Christian) Africans. Finally, we note that the only Muslim country with nuclear weapons (Pakistan) is financially all but bankrupt, socially divided, politically and militarily contained by India, and does not have the technology (thankfully, considering that country's internal instability) to deliver their weapons further than their regional opponents.

In short, Islam is the world's greatest paper tiger: fierce-looking, capable of being a nuisance, but on its own lacking real power.[II]

ORTHODOX ISLAM

Traditionally — and this held true from more or less the beginning of Islam up until around 1900—Islam was said to be split into two major doctrinal divisions (Sunni and Shi'a) and one minor one (Kharijites — the Ibadis being their much moderated descendants). The Sunnis comprised around 90 per cent of all Muslims, the Shi'a around 9 per cent, and the Ibadis less than 1 per cent. The Ibadis survived only in Oman and the Southern Sahara, the Shi'a were concentrated in Iran and Iraq (with some 'spill-over' into the Persian Gulf, Syria and Lebanon, Pakistan, India and Afghanistan), and the Sunnis everywhere else. The Sunnis were then split into four major schools of Islamic Law or *Madhhab*s (Hanafi, Hanbali, Maliki and Shafi'i) dating back to around 800 CE, and the Shi'a into two major *Madhhab*s (the Ja'faris — the so-called 'Twelvers' — and the

---

[II] The Prophet himself predicted this reversal in Islam's fortunes as follows: *'There will come a day when the [different] nations will fight you as if gulping down a meal.' Someone asked him: 'Will we be few then?' He answered 'No, you will be multitudes, but... [weak] like froth on a current'* (*Sunan Abu Dawud*, 'Kitab al-Malahim', n.4297). N.B. This is a prophetic narration (*hadith*) to which Usama bin Laden's Fatwa alludes (see Appendix I).

Zeidis — the so-called 'Fivers' — who, from earliest times, were concentrated in the Yemen).[12] These together formed the so-called 'seven *madhhabs*' of Islam. Mention must then be made of the Sufis and the students of *Irfan*. These are not followers of new legal schools — quite the contrary, the Sufis are fully Sunni, and the students of *Irfan* are fully Shi'a — but rather mystics within those legal schools: they are the Muslim equivalent of old monastic orders of Christianity and are the ascetics of Islam. They believe that in order to love and know God *fully* one should intensify prayer and abandon all worldliness, or even abandon the world altogether (as hermits). Among the Sufi Brotherhoods or *Turuq* (singular: *Tariqa*) are such famous orders as the Shadhiliyya, the Qadiriyya, the Rifa'iyya, the Mevleviyya (started by Jalal al-Din Rumi, and now famous in the West for their dancing and for Rumi's love poetry), the Naqshbandiyya, the Chistiyya, the Kubrawiyya, the Suhrawardiyya, the Tija-niyya, the Yashrutiyya, the Badawiyya and the Khalwatiyya. Indeed, it is estimated that in 1900, at least 25 per cent of all adult Sunni Muslims were either 'full adepts' of these and other Sufi orders (*murid*s) or informally associated with them (*mutabarrikin*).

All of the above together constitute *traditional Islamic Orthodoxy* (the word 'orthodox' coming from the Greek words *ortho* and *doxia* meaning 'correct opinion'). They all recognized each other as 'orthodox' and whilst often disagreeing with each other about specific issues there was a consensus between them that they all still belonged to the 'House of Islam' (*Dar al-Islam*).

[12] The so-called 'Seveners', or Isma'ilis, are not generally considered to be 'orthodox' due to their Gnostic Dualism, despite the high profiles in the West of the famous hereditary leaders of their Nizari branch, the Aga Khans. On the other hand, it should be mentioned that the Indian Dawudi Bohara — who are technically and historically an Isma'ili movement — are now considered orthodox, having re-adopted crucial Shafi'i and Ja'fari Shi'i tenets.

Conversely, they also all believed that tiny offshoot sects with strange doctrines such as the Druze, the (Isma'ili) Alawis (as opposed to the Alawi tariqa which is merely a branch of the great Shadhiliyya Sufi tariqa) the Shaykhis, the Bahais, the Babis, and the Ahmadiyya of Qadyan (all these sects together numbering less than the equivalent of 1 per cent of the orthodox) were 'heretics' and did not belong to the *House of Islam*.[13]

DIVISIONS WITHIN THE HOUSE

After around 1900 two radically new divisions entered the House of Islam for the first time in its history: 'Islamic Modernism' and 'Islamic Fundamentalism'. These were not legal or juridical divisions as such, but rather ideological ones, for they both rejected, in different ways, all the traditional divisions made above. Orthodox Islam largely ignored them,[14] but in their wake, or rather, under their influence, *Orthodox Islam* was unofficially renamed *Traditional Islam*, creating the **three major ideological divisions** that we have today: **Traditional Islam (Orthodox Islam), Islamic Modernism** and **Islamic Fundamentalism.**

---

[13] From the point of view of Orthodox Islam it need hardly be said that Elijah Mohammed's — and currently Louis Farrakhan's — 'Nation of Islam' is a radical American 'Black Nationalist' group which is not only doctrinally completely heretical (believing, as they do in a so-called twentieth-century 'prophet' called 'the Fard'), but also philosophically and culturally completely farcical. Unfortunately, however, most Americans — due to the group's high profile in the USA — lump the two together, much to the detriment of the image of Orthodox Islam. However, it must also be said that, whereas there are only about twenty thousand members of Farrakhan's 'Nation of Islam', there are at least a million black American Muslims, and thus Orthodox Islam is the rule rather than the exception amongst black American Muslims.

[14] Orthodox Islam was, despite its internal resilience and despite its inherent resistance to change, largely passive before them for the following reasons: (1) Orthodox Islam was for the first sixty years of the twentieth

The House of Islam

ISLAMIC 'MODERNISM'

As to Islamic 'Modernism', let it be said that it was born around the turn of the twentieth century in Ottoman Turkey and in Egypt almost simultaneously. It consisted of a 'reform movement' by politically-minded urbanites who had but scant knowledge of traditional Islam but had witnessed and studied Western technology and socio-political ideas, or even had actually visited the West. These people realized that the Islamic world was being 'left behind' technologically by the West and had become too weak to stand up to it. They blamed this weakness on what they saw as 'traditional Islam', which they thought 'held them back' and was not 'progressive' enough. They thus called for a complete 'overhaul' of Islam, including — or rather in particular — Islamic Law (*Shari'a*) and Doctrine (*'Aqida*). Despite some sentimental attachment to their religion and its culture, they basically felt that 'West is Best' and that Islam is something embarrassingly retrograde that needs to be constantly changed and 'updated'. They were also constantly 'apologizing'

---

century too pre-occupied with dealing with the ravages of Colonialism to deal with seemingly unimportant internal divisions. (2) Orthodox Islam is inherently 'unpoliticized', and so tends to ignore modern political ideologies. (3) The two great Institutes that traditionally unified and led the Sunni Islamic World — the Caliphate and the Azhar (the one temporal and the other scholarly) — in reaction to any threats against it were both eroded during the twentieth century: although the last Pan-Islamic Caliphate (the Ottoman Caliphate) was not officially abolished until 1924, it effectively came to an end with the Young Turks *coup* of 1908 and with the abdication of Sultan Abd al-Hamid II in 1909. Similarly, although the Azhar exists to this day and its Rector (the *Imam al-Akbar* or *Sheikh al-Azhar*) still maintains a certain prestige in the Sunni world, after its nationalization in the 1950s and 1960s by President Nasser of Egypt (which included making its Rector a government-appointed position), it lost its real credibility and status as the ultimate scholarly arbitrator of Sunni Islam.

for Islam so that the Qur'an for them went from being 'the Immutable Word of God' to 'humanistic philosophy advanced for its time'; Islamic prayer went from being 'the act of adoration of the Lord by the servant' to being 'primitive calisthenics', and fasting went from 'a sacred rite to dominate the ego and the body' to 'a practice that is good for the stomach', and so on. Needless to say, Modernism never really caught on popularly in the Islamic world, with the exception of Turkey where, from 1924 on, it was officially enforced by the secular leader Kamal Ataturk and his successors. However, even today the majority of the populace continues to be staunchly orthodox despite government policies. Indeed, until today 'Islamic Modernism' remains popularly the object of derision and ridicule, and is scorned by both traditional Muslims and fundamentalists alike. It did make gains, however, among some of the richer urban élites all over the Islamic world, many of whom had anyway been to the West to study and imbibed from it a secular perspective, not to say a completely different mental universe and mindset. Through them Modernism eventually came to be the dominant ideology in many, if not most, *governments* in Islamic countries. To this day, however, none of these governments, with the possible exception of that of Turkey, would ever dare to publicly or officially contradict the doctrines and beliefs of Orthodox Islam.

ISLAMIC FUNDAMENTALISM

Actually, the term 'fundamentalism' as applied to politicized, militant and iconoclastic religion is a misnomer, because Islam as such, and in fact all authentic religions, are *fundamentalist* in that they pertain to the fundamentals of life and of existence, and in that they engage both the body and soul of man. Nevertheless, the current meaning of the term is clear enough, as are its connotations of militancy, of being highly politicized and of its being something new and antithetical to the orthodox tradition.

In Islam, fundamentalism only gained significant ground during the twentieth century. It basically consists of **three separate movements**, two in the Sunni world[15] and one in the Shiʻa world: first, **Wahhabism/Salafism**, then the **Muslim Brotherhood** (*Ikhwan Muslimin*) and last '**Revolutionary Shiʻism**'.

We will return to the first of the Sunni forms of fundamentalism (Wahhabism/Salafism) shortly. As to the **Muslim Brotherhood**, it was founded in Egypt in 1928 by Sheikh Hasan al-Banna (1906–1949).[16] It started in theory as an organization for 'self-rectification' but soon developed into a full-scale social and political movement, involving itself in everything from political parties, labour unions and demonstrations, to building and owning religious schools, hospitals, banks, welfare societies

[15] Mention should perhaps also be made here of the militant 'Islamic' *Tahriri* (Liberation) Party, which was founded by the Sheikh al-Nabhani in 1951. This party focused on the call for the restitution (through violence and political struggle) of the Islamic Caliphate, and although it never spread to more than a few dozen hard-core members in every Islamic country, its name gained prominence for a while from 1960–1990 through its stridency, its violent methods and its attempts at internal agitation in the Arab world.

[16] Along with Hasan al-Banna we cannot fail to mention the prolific and fiery Egyptian ideologue Sayyid Qutb (1906–1966) who became (after Banna's assassination) the next greatest influence on the Muslim Brotherhood's thought and history. It was Qutb who first popularised the call for a *Jihad* against corrupt unIslamic governments of Muslim countries, before he was finally executed by the Egyptian state. Equally, mention must be made of Mawlana Mawdudi (1903–1979) who founded the influential Jamaʻat-i-Islami (Islamic Society) in (pre-partition) Pakistan in 1941 with much the same 'Islamic social reforms' aims as Hasan al-Banna and the pre-Qutb Muslim Brotherhood, but who remained, until his death, a milder figure, ultimately eschewing direct political violence.

and newspapers. It also at various points in time involved itself in more militaristic activities such as recruitment for international conflicts and physical training for the young. Until around 1980 it was the dominant form of fundamentalism in the Islamic world, but for all that it did not (apart from refocusing Islam on worldly political action and rejecting the temporal authority of the governments of Islamic countries) attempt to make any significant changes in Islamic doctrine or belief. In fact, the Muslim Brotherhood generally avoided doctrinal and spiritual issues altogether, focusing almost exclusively on worldly actions, and indeed built up a formidable network of semi-independent (from the Supreme Leadership in Egypt) political parties in almost every Islamic country in the world, with particular strongholds in the Arab World (but often under different local names, e.g. Hamas). They even came to power (starting in 1989) for a number of years in Sudan under the 'spiritual leadership' of Hasan Turabi (Speaker of the Parliament from 1997), but President Omar Bashir's dismissal of the Parliament in late 1999 signified the end of their stranglehold on that country.

Starting in around 1980, however, the Muslim Brotherhood became increasingly infiltrated by Wahhabi-Salafis. That is to say that many Salafis joined their ranks, and more and more of their members started to adopt Salafi doctrinal ideology. Moreover, because of their rule of 'staying away from (intra-Islamic) controversy' the Muslim Brotherhood began *de facto* accepting Wahhabi ideological positions (such as avoiding all mention of theology, philosophy, sacred art and mysticism in Islam, etc., as will be discussed later). Thus by the year 2000 the dominant unofficial ideology in the Brotherhood became Salafism, particularly in the 'up-and-coming' second and third tiers of their leadership structure, to the extent that in the coming 20 years the Salafis could quite possibly commandeer the Muslim Brotherhood movement altogether.

As to **'Revolutionary Shi'ism'** it has its doctrinal origin in Ayatollah Khomeini's doctrine of *Vilayet i-Faqih*, first published in the early 1960s. This doctrine basically said that (Shi'a) Muslims should not obey the worldly authorities — as traditional Shi'ism had always held, whilst awaiting the prophesized Mahdi[17] — but rather that they should obey Shi'a clerics who should themselves hold all temporal power. This doctrine was revolutionary and fundamentalist because, for the first time in the history of Shi'ism, it stated that nobody was fit to rule who was not a Shi'a cleric. However, the idea would have remained an anomaly in the dust-bin of history had not Ayatollah Khomeini swept to power in Iran in 1979 and established the Islamic Republic of Iran on the basis of that idea. Thus Shi'a fundamentalism began, for all intents and purposes, in 1979, and is synonymous with the Islamic Republic of Iran and the Iranian Revolution.

THE RISE OF WAHHABISM

Wahhabism has its origins in the iconoclastic ideas of the Najdi preacher Muhammad 'Abd al-Wahhab (1703–1787) — hence the name *'Wahhabi'*. 'Abd al-Wahhab claimed to be 'purifying Islam of innovations' by drawing on the teachings of the Syrian jurist Ibn Taymiyya (1263–1328; it will be noted Ibn Taymiyya himself came a full 700 years after Islam's formative period), and for a while, in political alliance with a local Bedouin family later to be known as the House of Sa'ud, created a Bedouin military rebellion in Central Arabia. That rebellion was eventually

---

[17] The Mahdi is a great Muslim spiritual leader foretold by the Prophet himself as coming at the end of time and heralding the Second Coming of Christ.

quashed by a combination of the Ottoman Caliphate, the Mamluk rulers of Egypt and the Hashemite rulers of the Hijaz. 'Abd al-Wahhab's ideas would also have been consigned to historical obscurity, had not a Bedouin leader descended from 'Abd al-Wahhab's original ally (Muhammad Ibn Sa'ud) raised 'Abd al-Wahhab's standard again 150 years later. This time the movement fared better, for under the Wahhabi banner, Ibn Sa'ud's descendent, 'Abd al-'Aziz bin Sa'ud, through his great personal courage, physical strength and military prowess, united the Bedouin tribes of Central Arabia,[18] defeated his Arab rivals in the Arabian Peninsula (including, this time, the Hashemites of Mecca) and formed the Kingdom of Saudi Arabia (1932) with himself as its first king. Ever since the newly-founded Saudi Arabia signed an oil concession with Standard Oil of California (Chevron) in May 1933, Saudi money has consistently flowed to Wahhabi coffers, and Wahhabism started spreading all over the Islamic world.

This growth remained more or less incremental, however, until around the early 1970s when three factors combined to boost Saudi, and consequently Wahhabi, prestige: (1) the death of the charismatic President Nasser of Egypt and the subsequent political bankruptcy of the ideology of pan-Arab union and Arab nationalism; (2) the successful use of an Oil Embargo against the West by Saudi King Faisal in 1973, following the October 1973 Arab-Israeli War; and (3) the huge increase of oil revenues to the Middle East, in particular to Saudi Arabia, the world's biggest oil-exporter (with over one quarter of the world's proven oil reserves). Indeed, it is highly significant to

---

[18] Ibn Sa'ud's Bedouin contingents were also, like the Muslim Brotherhood, called the *Ikhwan* or 'Brothers', but had nothing to do with the latter. In Arabic, they are usually distinguished by calling the former quite simply the '*Ikhwan*' and the latter the '*Ikhwan Muslimin*' ('the Muslim Brothers').

note that in 1969 the OIC (Organization of the Islamic Conference—the Muslim 'UN', as it were) was established with its
General Secretariat in Jeddah, Saudi Arabia, and that it has
been dominated by Saudi Arabia ever since. It is even more
significant to note that in 1973 a decision was taken at the OIC
to create an Islamic Development Bank (which became opera-
tional in 1975) whereby the poorer Islamic countries would be
financially assisted by (mainly) Saudi Arabia.

The most recent quantum leap in the rate of Wahhabi expansion came after 1979, when alarmed on the one hand, by the
Soviet invasion of Afghanistan and, on the other hand, by the
Iranian Revolution and the growth of Shi'i fundamentalism,
the USA (under the Reagan administration), Pakistan and Saudi
Arabia formed an unspoken alliance to check both threats. The
alliance's strategy was to everywhere burgeon their support
for Wahhabi ideology and the Wahhabi movement in general,
and even to create an international Wahhabi proxy army to fight
the Soviets in Afghanistan. The USA is said to have given
the blessing and planning for this operation; Pakistan provided
the logistics, supplied the weapons, made available the military
training bases, and organized Salafi Islamic schools (or madrasas)
to call for an international *Jihad;* Saudi Arabia provided the
funds, the preachers and the ideology; and the manpower came
from all over the Islamic World. This was the Cold War era —
the era of the 'good' (because they were fighting the Soviets)
Afghan *Mujahidin* ('Holy Warrior') and the Iran-Contra scandal
— and it was during this time that the most radical Wahhabis
(called *Takfiris*) became armed and independently organized.
Usama bin Laden was one of these *Mujahids* and he received
his formative military and logistical training in the Afghani war.
In this sense the attacks on September 11th were an ironic and
tragic case of 'blowback' for the USA. The apogee of this period

of intensified Saudi-funded Wahhabi ascendancy was symboli-
cally marked in 1986 when King Fahd of Saudi Arabia took on
the additional title of 'Custodian of the Two Holy Mosques' (in
Mecca and Medina), reminding the whole Islamic world under
whose power the two holy cities lay.

Today it is estimated that whilst less than 1 per cent of
Muslims are deliberately and consciously Wahhabi (and opposed to traditional Islam) in their outlook,[19] the Wahhabis nevertheless influence or reach with their ideas about 10 per cent of
all Sunnis. It is thought, moreover, that these percentages are
only likely to rise with time unless the governments of Muslim
States make a deliberate effort to check them.

One final note is that the 'Wahhabis' are generally called
'Wahhabis' in Saudi Arabia and (since around 1980) 'Salafis'
outside of that country, albeit that they are in reality exactly the
same group, holding exactly the same views. The term *Salafi* [20]
comes from the Arabic term *Salaf* meaning 'past', but is a
misnomer, because, as will be seen in the following chapter, the
'Salafis' do anything but harken back to the past, and reject the
vast majority of Islam's intellectual heritage, development and
historical experience, albeit whilst claiming to 'go back' to
(what in their imagination) was seventh-century Arabia.

---

[19] The only countries in the world that are *officially* Wahhabi or Salafi are
Saudi Arabia and Qatar. Afghanistan under the Taliban was too. Although
the Taliban were initially mainly Deobandi hardliners, under Mulla Omar
they soon dove-tailed with Salafism.

[20] The original Salafi movement, or rather the movement which first
used that name, was not Fundamentalist at all, but (ironically) Modernist:
they were in fact the first 'Modernist Reformers' of Egypt at the beginning
of the twentieth century; their leaders being the Mufti Muhammad 'Abduh
and Jamal al-Din al-Afghani.

The Salafi Ideology,
Doctrines and Tenets:
What do they Believe?

T HE WAHHABI-SALAFIS have a number of doctrines, tenets
and even practices that are completely new and unique to
them, and that have never before been taken seriously in the
history of Islam. Many of these contradict some of the most fun-
damental tenets of the Islamic faith, and involve some inherently complex doctrinal issues. In what follows, however, we
will endeavour to summarize these for the reader without over-
simplification or inaccuracies.

I. REJECTION OF TRANSMITTED KNOWLEDGE
(*Naql*) AND OF THE AUTHORITY OF THE CANON

The Salafis reject not just the very notion of an Islamic Canon
but also all of its texts in their traditional form with the exception of the Holy Qur'an. They also reject transmitted knowledge (*naql:* that is, the sum total of what Muslims have thought,
said and accepted over history and the sum total of Islamic historical experience) by saying: 'We are men and they are men'
(*Nahnu rijal wa hum rijal*, meaning 'as we are all men why
should we accept that anyone else knows better than us?'). This
leaves 'the door open' for them, as it were, to reinvent Islam in
whatever form they want.

2. REJECTION OF THE SOURCES OF LAW
(*Usul al-Fiqh*)

The Salafis reject the traditional Principles of Jurisprudence (*Usul al-fiqh*). These Principles of Jurisprudence are the very sources and foundations of Islamic Holy Law (*Shari'a*); they determine how Islamic Law is formulated. Specifically, these are four: (1) The Holy Qur'an; (2) *Hadith* (the corpus of sayings of the Prophet) and *Sunna* (what is recorded of the Prophet's actions); (3) *Qiyas* (logical free analogy based on principles found in Qur'an and *Hadith*); and (4) *Ijma'* (the unanimous consensus of the qualified scholars of the Muslim nation or *Umma*). This is to say that Islamic scholars, when formulating the *Shari'a* on a specific issue, first look in the Qur'an to see if there is anything specifically about that issue; if there is nothing applicable there they then look in the *Hadith* corpus to see if the Prophet said anything about that issue, or undertook a specific action in a context pertaining to that issue;[21] if there is nothing there they extrapolate principles (through *Qiyas*) from the afore-mentioned two sources and apply them to a new context (e.g. since alcohol is banned because it hurts not just the drinker but also his family and community, therefore drugs too are banned for the same reason); then, finally, if they cannot find a clear and applicable precedent, all the *qualified* Islamic scholars (*'ulama*) meet and form a consensus (*Ijma'*) about a topic, taking into consideration above all the general good.[22]

[21] What the Prophet said and did is considered authoritative because the Qur'an, the Word of God, says: *Obey God and His messenger* (3:32 et al.), and: *Whatsoever the messenger permitteth you, take it. And whatsoever he forbiddeth you, abstain (from it)* (59:7). Likewise, the Prophet is to be emulated because the Qur'an says: *Verily in the messenger of God ye have a good example for whosoever hopeth in God ...* (33:21).

[22] *Ijma'* is considered authoritative because the Prophet had said: *My*

The Salafi Ideology

In what follows we will dwell on these points in more detail, but it suffices to note here that in rejecting the traditional concept of *Usul al-fiqh*, the Salafis are setting into motion the making of an entirely new sacred law or *Shari'a* and therefore ultimately the making of an entirely different civilization. They are re-opening the door of 'absolute' or 'unconditional' *Ijtihad* (new opinion)[23] in *Usul al-fiqh*, without knowing where it will lead.

---

nation will never be wrong when they have a consensus (*Sunan Ibn Maja*, 2: 1303, n.3950 et al.), and: *The Hand of God is with consensus* (*Jami' al-Tirmidhi*, hadith hasan).

[23] **The 'Door' of *Ijtihad*.**
There seems to be a lot of confusion among Western scholars and even Muslims writers about the question of 're-opening' the 'door' of *Ijtihad*: in fact 'the door of' (i.e. the permissibility of) particular *Ijtihad* (i.e. *Ijtihad* on particular issues) has never been closed *de jure*. Admittedly, at one moment in time some Muslim scholars thought that all possible issues had been addressed — and so there was no need *de facto* for new particular *Ijtihad* — but the emergence of new technologies after the Renaissance (and increasingly since the twentieth century) completely disproved this idea, since these technologies gave rise to new questions.

What has been 'closed' until Muhammad bin 'Abd al-Wahhab is *Ijtihad* about *Usul al-fiqh* in general or 'absolute *Ijtihad*' — i.e. *Ijtihad* about what the very sources of Law should be, and the freedom to judge independently of them based only upon the Qur'an and the *Hadith*. This, however, is precisely what 'Abd al-Wahhab did and is obviously something radically different from 'ordinary *Ijtihad*'. To be considered qualified to do this, and thereby be a *Mujtahid*, one had to: (1) have mastered the Arabic language, its dialects, its proverbs and classical poetry. (2) Have a complete grasp of *Fiqh*, its sources, the different *Madhhab*s and their arguments, and to have practised being a legal judge (*Qadi*) on their basis. (3) Know the Qur'an by heart including all seven vocal recitations, and have fully mastered the sciences of *Tafsir* and interpretation. (4) Have mastered the *Hadith* completely. (Ibn Hanbal himself had memorized all 600,000 different *Hadith*s ever reported up to the ninth century — and could distinguish between the true ones and the false ones — but said that a *Mujtahid* need only have memorized 400,000!) (5) Be scrupulously pious in religion, beloved in his

23

3. REJECTION OF THE SCIENCES OF LANGUAGE
AND INTERPRETATION

Words change over time, or rather, what is understood by certain words changes over time, as peoples and cultures change and develop. For example, the words 'being' or 'essence' or 'form' (to say nothing of more casual words like 'hot' or 'cool') in English do not mean the same thing nowadays as they did one hundred years ago. For a civilization based essentially upon a written text (the Holy Qur'an) this could pose a potential problem over time: how to know if what contemporary Arabs understand by this or that word is the same as what was understood by that same word in seventh-century Arabia?

Muslim scholars traditionally overcame this problem in two ways: by studying the origins or *etymology* of the Arabic language and by taking as linguistic references for Qur'anic words pre-Islamic *Jahiliyya* poetry (a large body of which is extant, and which is of a very high linguistic order). In other words, Muslim scholars 'fix' the meanings of words (etymologically) by studying their origins[24] and (semantically) by studying how they were used and what they meant just before Islam. The Salafis of course reject this — without understanding it at all, it must be said — on the grounds that pre-Islamic poetry is pagan

community, upstanding in conduct and so on. Needless to say only a handful of people in Islamic history have ever fulfilled these conditions, and 'Abd al-Wahhab certainly was *not* one of them.

[24] Almost every word in Arabic can be reduced to a 'root word' consisting of three letters, and each of these 'root words' takes its meaning from a natural phenomenon, which in turn is identified by one of its qualities. Thus, for example, the Arabic word for passionate love (*'ishq*) takes its name from a certain desert plant that grows over another plant so that gradually the two become one: love was seen to have that quality and so it was given that name. Now obviously this science (Arabic etymology) is of tremendous value when trying to determine the classical or original meaning of words.

and therefore worthless. Consequently, they can change the meanings of words as they please. For example, in a famous *Hadith* the Prophet said: *In the Najd is sedition and the horns of the devil will emerge from it.*[25] Now the Najd is in the eastern part of the Saudi Arabian desert and Riyadh is its capital, and it is called that now and was called that at the time of the Prophet — and indeed most traditional Muslims take this *Hadith* as referring precisely to 'Abd al-Wahhab and Wahhabism (see also Appendix II) — but because the Wahhabi-Salafis reject linguistic references they are able to say that the 'Najd' in question here is actually Iraq!

A similar thing happens as regards the rules of interpretation of the Qur'an (the traditional Sciences of Exegesis and Hermeneutics). Without going into this too deeply — we only mention it in the first place because it has direct, concrete consequences — we note that it was always believed that the Qu'ran cannot be interpreted correctly without knowing the rules of its interpretation. These rules are as follows: that one must first know the historical context for each verse (*asbab al-nuzul*); that there is no redundancy (*taraduf*) in the Qur'an; that one has to explain one verse *together* with other relevant verses (*al-Qur'an ba'duhu yufassir ba'd*); that some verses are abrogated

---

Incidentally, this science explains why grammarians always joke that 'every word in Arabic has something to do with a camel!': every word goes to a root which in turn goes back to a natural phenomenon, and since nature for the Arabs was the desert, and the centrepiece of the desert was the camel, it is easy to see why a lot of words in Arabic do have something to do with a camel

[25] For references to this *Hadith* and to thirty others like it about Najd, see: Al-Sayyid al-Alawi bin Ahmad al-Haddad's *Misbah al-Anam wa Jala' al-Zalam fi Radd Shubah al-Bid'i al-Nadi al-lati adalla biha al-'Awamm* (1325 AH); see also Appendix II.

by others (*nasikh wa mansukh*); that there is a difference between a general ruling (*'amm*) and a particular ruling (*khass*), and between a qualified one (*muqayyad*) and an unqualified one (*mutlaq*), and so on. The importance of interpreting the Qur'an according to these rules would seem to be a fairly straightforward concept, yet the Salafis reject it blindly and thoughtlessly, and consequently 'open the door' to completely random interpretations of the Qur'an.

4. REJECTION OF QUR'ANIC COMMENTARIES (*Tafsir*)

Classical Qur'anic commentary (*Tafsir*) was one of the greatest endeavours in human intellectual history. There are hundreds of orthodox classical commentaries, some of them consisting of tens of thousands of pages. Qur'anic commentators asked every conceivable question and examined every imaginable answer. Discussions on a single point or word (let alone verse or chapter) can last up to a hundred pages. Commentators even wrote in states of inspiration — in ecstatic visions or trances — and composed poetry in their commentaries to discuss issues. Anyone vaguely familiar with the corpus of classical *Tafsir* cannot fail to be intellectually astounded by them.

Yet of course the Salafis reject this corpus, sometimes just ignoring it and sometimes just being ignorant of it. They stick to paltry recent *Tafsir*s that hardly go beyond clarifying speaker and context (and that not always correctly). The pretext they give for this is that these texts contain Biblical references (*'Israiliyat'*), and they even use this excuse to disregard Tabari (whose *Tafsir* is one of the earliest and most comprehensive, and had been regarded, by Sunnis and even many Shi'a to be the most authoritative). Now two thirds of the Qur'an consists of stories recapitulating the lives of the Hebrew

Prophets and of Jesus and Mary, and a number of the Prophet's own companions were rabbis or monks who had become Muslims, so it makes no sense to disregard Biblical wisdom and references, especially when, as already quoted, it is an article of faith in the Qur'an to recognize both the Old and New Testaments as previous Scriptures.

Some Salafis go so far as to say that all interpretations of the Qur'an, except theirs, are wrong. This is the strongest possible proof of both their hubris and their monstrous ignorance since, after all, the Qur'an is, notwithstanding the verses that pertain to legal rulings (*ahkam*), a self-declared 'open text' which encourages people to deliberate its parables, lessons and wisdom. Moreover, there are Salafis who will even say that there is no good in the Qur'an except through their own interpretations of it. Indeed, the Salafi Sheikh Abd al-Rahim al-Tahhan said, in one of his recorded and publicly distributed sermons: 'There is no good in the Qur'an without the *Sunna* (the example of the Prophet), and there is no good in the *Sunna* without our righteous Salafi understanding of it' (*La khayra fi qur'an bi-ghayri sunna, wa la khayra fi sunna bi-ghayri fahm salafna al-salih*). The reason why this is completely heretic — aside from the fact that it reduces God's Knowledge to their knowledge and gives them a monopoly on God that God Himself has *de jure* no right to bypass! — is that it denies the ontological reality of the Qur'an according to the Qur'an itself. As mentioned earlier, for Muslims the Qur'an is Divine Revelation (*Tanzil*) and the Divine Word 'clothed' in the Arabic language (*Kalam Allah; Qur'anan Arabiyy*) and therefore has an incalculable reality (*Wujud*), a presence (*Hudur*) and a blessing (*Baraka*). To say there is no good in the Qur'an *in and of itself*, except through a given understanding of it, is thus to deny that it is Revelation, and also runs contrary to the practice of 80 per cent of the

Muslims of the world who do not understand Arabic and yet recite it regularly for its blessings and its beauty.

This evidently compounds the risk of arbitrary and random interpretation of the Qur'an. But for all that the Salafis are able to do only limited damage with these random interpretations, because on the whole the Qur'an is generally very clear in Arabic. They thus do not concentrate on the Qur'an as much as do traditional Muslims.

5. CHANGING THE SAYINGS
OF THE PROPHET (*Hadith*)

The *Hadith*, however, is where the Salafis do their real damage. The *Hadith* corpus has been 'fixed' by the eight traditional *Hadith* collections (mentioned earlier, in the section on the Canon) dating back from the ninth century. These collections of *Hadith* were selected less than 200 years after the Prophet's death with the greatest of care, each *Hadith* having a chain of narrators going back to the Prophet himself, and each *Hadith* (and its narrators) being historically, linguistically and logically scrutinized with the greatest care before its inclusion in any canonical collection.

The Salafis, in order to make the *Hadith* say what they want, have a process whereby their 'scholars' systematically but inscrutably 'correct' these ninth-century collections (apparently having a better idea now about what the Prophet said, and how he lived, than those who were only three or four eye-witnesses away from him). The most famous of these Salafi *Hadith* 'experts', Nasr al-Din al-Albani, died only in the year 2000 and was a watchmaker from Damascus with no formal training in the Islamic Sciences. However, thanks to him and his successors and students (such as Ali Hasan al-Halabi, Abd al-Qadir Arnaouti and Shu'ayb Arnaouti) — and of course to millions of Salafi dollars which print and give away his books free all over the world — the Salafis now have an entire 'revised' corpus of *Hadith* that says exactly what they want it to. Needless to say, moreover, this revised corpus is one that paves the way for a radical and politicized reinterpretation of Islam.

6. REJECTION OF ANALOGY (*Qiyas*), REASON AND THE LAWS OF LOGIC

Of all Salafi ideas, the rejection of 'free analogy' (*Qiyas*) is the only one with some precedent within traditional Islam: Ahmad ibn Hanbal, the founder of the Hanbali *Madhhab*, rejected *Qiyas* on the grounds that it was subjective since one could find apparently contradictory statements in the Qur'an and in the *Hadith*.[26] Now this question obviously hinges upon the concept of what is a 'logical dialectic', and is too complex for the present discussion, but suffice to say that Ibn Hanbal did not categorically reject reason or the laws of logic, whereas the Salafis do.[27]

---

[26] Ibn Hanbal was, however, the only founder of a *Sunni Madhhab* to reject *Qiyas*, and his *Madhhab* is the only one that continues to do so.

[27] **The Laws of Logic in Orthodox Islam.**

In orthodox Islam, on the other hand, logic is seen as reflecting the Divine Nature Itself: all logic is based upon two simple chief laws, the *Law of Contradiction* and the *Law of Excluded Middle*. The *Law of Contradiction* says that a proposition (*tarh*) *cannot be* both true *and* false at the same time and in the same respect, and that something cannot both be and not be, or have a quality and not have it, at the same time and in the same respect. The *Law of Excluded Middle* says that a proposition *must* either be true *or* false, and that something must either be or not be, and either have a particular quality or not have it. Thus in Orthodox Islam the *Law of Contradiction* is true because it asserts the absoluteness (*mutlaqiyya*) of truth — that something either *is* or *is not* — and thus reflects the Absoluteness of God (for truth comes from God; the Holy Qur'an says: *That is because God is the*

7. REJECTION OF CONSENSUS (*Ijma'*)

As explained, *Ijma'* is the consensus of Muslims on a given issue and was sanctioned by the Prophet himself. The Salafis, following Ibn Taymiyya and disregarding orthodox opinion, reject *Ijma'*. This is very convenient for them because it means they do not have to pay any attention to what anyone else thinks. It gives them the right to be **undemocratic.**

8. REJECTION OF THE PREREQUISITES OF MAKING NEW FATWAS

Whilst not as rigorous as the prerequisites for making 'absolute' *Ijtihad*, there are nevertheless stringent traditional prerequisites of religious knowledge (including knowing the Qur'an by heart, knowing *Fiqh*, knowing *Hadith*, understanding the rules of interpretation and being a practising Muslim of fine standing in the community) required for making a *Fatwa* (a religious edict or ruling, based upon existing opinions). Needless to say that few of the Salafi Sheikhs that issue Fatwas all over the world on a daily basis meet these pre-conditions, and the Salafis do not believe they are required to in the first place.

9. LITERALISM

The Holy Qur'an says: *He it is who hath revealed unto thee (Muhammad) the Scripture wherein are clear revelations — they are the substance of the Book — and others (which are) allegorical . . .* (3:7)

Truth! Lo! He quickeneth the dead, and lo! He is Able to do all things (22:6)). Thus equally in Orthodox Islam the *Law of Excluded Middle* is true because it asserts the infinitude (*la niha'iyya*) of truth — that there are *no other possibilities other than something either being or not being* — which itself reflects the Infinitude of God.

There are thus two kinds of verses in the Qur'an: verses that are literal ('clear' — these are the ones from which the *Shari'a* is derived), and verses which are allegorical (not unlike Jesus's parables) or 'inherently open to *reasonable* interpretation' (these being the ones from which Islamic wisdom and culture is derived). Of the latter type the Qur'an says repeatedly: *God speaketh to mankind in allegories…* (24:35) and: *God coineth the similitudes for mankind in order that they may reflect…* (14:25).

Yet despite this the Salafis somehow manage to say that there is no allegory (*Majaz*) in the Qur'an, and that every word in the Qur'an must *be taken literally*. The great champion of this idea, the late Sheikh Bin Baz (who was the Head of *Idarat Hayat al-Buhuth wal Da'wa wal-Irshad* in Riyadh and was himself blind) was mischievously asked by one of his students, if there was no *Majaz* in the Qur'an, what did he make of the following verse: *Whosoever is blind in this world will be blind in the next world and yet further from the Way* (17:72)?

Again, this issue is not merely an academic one, but one that has direct consequences for Muslim behaviour and therefore on human life.

10. ANTHROPOMORPHISM (*Tajsim*)

The Prophet, in agreement with the Book of Genesis,[28] said: *Verily God created Adam in His own image.*[29] The Salafis, by contrast, are *anthropomorphic:* that is, they remake God in *their own* image. They believe that God is on His Throne in Heaven like a man, since the Qur'an describes that He has a *Hand*, a *Side*, a *Face*, a *Throne*, and that He is the *Hearer*, the *Seer* and so on. This idea is partly a result of the previous point

[28] *Genesis* 1:27: *God created man in His own image.*
[29] *Musnad Ibn Hanbal*, 2:244, 251, 315, 323 etc.; *Sahih Bukhari*, 'Kitab al-Isti'than', ch.1.

(literalism) and partly due to Ibn Taymiyya, who referring to a famous *Hadith*, once declared: 'God descends from the Heavens, even as I am descending from this *minbar* (pulpit)'.

Thus, instead of believing that man is made in God's image the Salafis believe that God is like a man sitting in the sky. They ignore the Qur'an's (and consequently the traditional Islamic) concept of a simultaneous and dialectical double analogy of *Tanzih* (abstraction) and *Tashbih* (similarity) between man and God: if on the one hand man reflects God's Attributes (being made in His image) and if God describes Himself in terms man can easily understand, then, on the other hand, God is also simultaneously infinitely beyond all comparisons. The Qur'an clearly expresses this dialectic 'double analogy' as follows: *Nothing is like unto Him, and He is the Hearer, the Seer* (42:11).

This issue has many subtle and often unspoken ramifications, the least of which being a general change of emphasis from spiritual matters onto worldly matters, and consequently on to politics: if God is exactly like a man, only All-powerful and sitting in the sky, then what men do here on earth and what happens in the world supersedes traditional spiritual matters such as worship and virtue.

II. DIMINUTION OF THE IMPORTANCE OF THE PROPHET, HIS FAMILY AND DESCENDENTS

Muslims traditionally have great reverence and veneration for the Prophet. This is evidently sanctioned by the Qur'an which says: *Lo! Thou (Muhammad) art of a tremendous nature* (68:4); and: *Verily God and His Angels shower blessings on the Prophet, Oh ye who believe! Invoke blessings on him and salute him with a worthy salutation* (33:56).

Consequently, Muslims (and especially Shi'a) also have a certain reverence and love for the Prophet's family and descendents.

The Qur'an says: *God's wish is but to remove uncleanness far from you, O Folk of the Household (of the Prophet) and purify you with a thorough purification* (33:33), and: *Say (O Muhammad, unto mankind): I ask of you no fee therefore, save loving kindness among kinsfolk* (42:23).

Finally, Muslims traditionally recognized that God has 'friends' from among the most pious believers (especially among the descendents of the Prophet and among the Sufis), this being the Muslim equivalent of a saint, except that in Islam there is no 'Church sanction' for these, so that God Himself decides who they are (based upon their faith and their deeds), although Muslim popular consensus may identify them. The Qur'an says: *God is the Friend of those who (truly) believe* (2:257).

By contrast, the Salafis diminish the role of the Prophet,[30] have no particular respect (to say nothing of active suspicion and hatred) for his descendents, and do not recognize saints. Of the Prophet they say 'Muhammad is a just a courier who delivered a message and died', and 'Abd al-Wahhab himself let one of his followers say, in his presence (and thus with his approval): 'My cane is better than Muhammad because it is useful in killing snakes and similar reptiles, whereas Muhammad is of no more use; he is just a courier and he passed away.'[31] Needless to say the Qur'an (and orthodox Islam) does not agree: *And call not those who are slain in the Way of God 'dead'. Nay, they are living, only ye perceive not* (2:154).

As to the Prophet's descendents (the Hashemites), it suffices

---

[30] The Mufti of Saudi Arabia, Sheikh 'Abd al-'Aziz Aal al-Sheikh, even went so far as to declare (by Fatwa) on May 22nd, 2002 that the traditional Islamic celebrations of the Prophet's birthday (*Mawlid al-Nabawi*) were heretical!

[31] Al-Sheikh Abu Na'im Radwan al-'Adl Baybars, *Rawdat al-Muhtajin li Ma'rifat Qawa'id al-Din* (1971), pp.384–385.

to say that 'Abd al-Wahhab and his heirs were continually at war with them when these ruled the Hijaz.

Finally, as to the idea of saints, they regard this as the very essence of polytheism (*shirk*), and it is perhaps the single thing they most despise. These ideas evidently have political implications as through them the Wahhabi-Salafis free themselves of the need to respect rulers and scholars descended from the Prophet, and the mystical masters of *Tasawwuf* (Sufism).

12. REJECTION OF THEOLOGY (*Ilm al-Kalam*)

The Salafis reject theology completely. They even say that it is forbidden and a sin to ask about God's Attributes and Nature. However, the Qur'an is replete with references to the Divine Names and Qualities, such as the following:

> *He is the First and the Last, and the Outward and the Inward; and He is Knower of all things* (57:3).

> *He is God other than Whom there is no god, the King, the Holy One, the Great Peace, the Keeper of Faith, the Guardian, the Majestic, the Compeller, the Superb. Glorified be God from all that they ascribe as partner (unto Him)* (59:23).

The Salafis, however, say these Names and Qualities must be accepted without asking questions (*'bila kayf'*), and that one should not even think about why different Divine Qualities and Names are specified in the Qur'an, as if the Qur'an says things gratuitously.

13. REJECTION OF PHILOSOPHY

The Salafis reject philosophy, even — or perhaps especially — religious philosophy based on theology (philosophy was often traditionally described as 'the handmaiden of theology'). They regard it all as sinful and mere sophistry.

14. REJECTION OF MYSTICISM

Connected to the Salafi rejection of sanctity is their rejection of — and hatred for — Islamic Mysticism (*Tasawwuf*), whose goal was, precisely, sanctity and total inward purification, as in the mysticisms of other religions. They regard the Sufis as their mortal enemies, both doctrinally and individually. They even reject traditional 'spiritual psychology', based on the Qur'an, that tries to cure the soul of faults, bad habits, vices and so on, because for them all that matters is outward obedience.

15. REJECTION OF SACRED ART

The Prophet said: *Verily God is Beautiful and loveth beauty.*[32] For over a thousand years Muslims have been making sacred art on that basis — including some of the most beautiful art the world has ever seen, from the architecture of the Great Mosque at Cordoba and the Taj Mahal, to the Qur'anic illumination and calligraphy of Ibn al-Bawwab; from Persian and Baluchi carpets, to Egyptian chanting of the Qur'an and to the blue robes of the Tuaregs.

The Salafis reject the concept of sacred art — the concept of an art that by reflecting the Divine Nature in geometrical principles, symbolic content, formal harmony and stylistic perfection aims to predispose the soul to spiritual contemplation and purity. Equally, they reject the concept of traditional music which, through melody and rhythm, aims to induce in the soul peace and love of beauty (and consequently of Divine Beauty and thus of the Divine Itself).

Consequently, since even Salafis are necessarily surrounded by forms, they end up using profane art or simply ugly or artless

---

[32] *Musnad Ibn Hanbal,* ch.4:122; 124; and 151.

things: they make mosques that look like giant concrete match-boxes; they shout the *Adhan* (call to prayer) over microphones rather than chant it in harmony; they sit on western mass-produced sofas in their mosques instead of the traditional hand-carved minbars; they fill their houses with Asian factory-made goods rather than local traditional handcrafts; and they decorate their homes with gaudy propaganda posters rather than traditional calligraphy. This attitude not only reflects, but also psychologically perpetuates, their rejectionism and spiritual impoverishment in other areas.

16. REJECTION OF LEGAL SCHOOLS (*Madhhabs*) AND ILL-TREATMENT OF TRADITIONAL MUSLIMS AND MINORITIES

In every pan-Islamic conference, or whenever a Salafi discusses *Fiqh* with a traditional Muslim, the Salafis raise the slogan 'Islam without *Madhhabs*' ('*Al-Islam bila Madhahib*'). What this actually means is 'our *madhhab* without discussion'! The Salafis say they do not believe in *Madhhabs* in Islam and really mean that they do not believe in — or even respect — anybody else's *Madhhab* in Islam. Moreover, they do not even respect *the persons* of Muslims who believe in *Madhhabs* (i.e. traditional Muslims). Consequently they oppress traditional Muslims who fall under their power. One need only consider the treatment of the Shi'a at the hands of Wahhabi-Salafi Sheikhs in Saudi Arabia or in Afghanistan under the Taliban (1996–2001) to appreciate the extent of this.

17. WOMEN'S RIGHTS

Salafi suppression of women's rights is well known: they do not let them work (except in all-female environments); they do not let them drive; they do not let them go out of the house without an adult male member of the family (*mahram*) to accompany them; they give themselves the right to beat them at the drop of a hat; they force them to cover their faces with black veils; they do not let them participate in the any government affairs or in the decision-making process (and often not even in making their own decisions); and, in Afghanistan under the Taliban, they did not allow them to be educated. Needless to say *none* of these are beliefs or practices to be found in Orthodox Islam.

18. MARRIAGE

Marriage is the central institution of family life and society, and thus the central institution of Orthodox Islam. The Prophet said: *Marriage is half of religion, so [you who are already married] fear God in the other half.* [33]

In Orthodox Sunni Islam there are five conditions for a legal marriage: (1) that there be a proposal; (2) that the proposal be accepted (*by the woman herself, or by someone she permits to speak for her*, usually her father); (3) that both parties agree on the amount of a 'bridal price' which the groom gives the bride upon marriage, and a 'divorce price' which he gives her should they get divorced; (4) that there be two witnesses to this 'marriage contract'; and (5) that both parties have the *intention* of a permanent marriage (even if they later change their minds and get a divorce). There are also all sorts of rights that a woman has over her husband once she is married (and of course vice versa), most notably that the husband not be allowed to touch any of the wife's monies or properties once they are married, including the 'bridal price' itself (even if she be richer than him), and that he take care of all of the household and family

---

[33] Abu Hamid al-Ghazali, *Ihya' 'Ulum al-Din*, ch.3, 14.

expenses, including feeding her and clothing her in the same style and expense that he feed and clothe himself. The man is also obliged to make time for his wife and children.

The Salafis cut short many of these conditions and rights including the *intention* of permanence (some traditional Shi'a do this as well) and including a woman's rights after she is married. Thus, in the Salafi *Zawaj Sirri* ('secret marriage') there are two witnesses to the marriage but these are sworn to — or intimidated into — secrecy, so that the marriage remains secret even from the husband's own relatives (and husbands can thus have other wives[34] and children at their will — in such cases brothers and sisters routinely go through their whole lives without knowing of each other's existence!). Similarly, in the Salafi *Zawaj Misyar* ('marriage without dowry or rights'), a woman has no right to live with her husband, and a man can just visit that woman at her home, whenever he pleases, and does not have to feed her or clothe her, etc. (and does not even have to tell anyone about it if the *Zawaj Misyar* is also a *Zawaj Sirri*).

---

34 **Polygamy.**

The Qur'an allows (but discourages 4:3; 4:129) polygamy up to four wives, so that traditionally it was generally thought that a man should not take more than one wife unless there were 'extraordinary circumstances', these generally being one of the following: (1) that a man's first wife be barren, and he wish to have children and yet not want to divorce his first wife or cast her out; (2) that a man's brother be dead and that he wish — out of charity — to raise his fatherless nephews and nieces in his own house, and therefore marry their widowed mother so that they might all live together under one roof; (3) that the first wife be very ill or permanently incapacitated and that the husband not be able to cope alone with work and with children; (4) that a ruler need to take more than one wife, from different political factions, in order to appease them; (5) that there be, after a period of extended war or disease, a severe shortage of men in a land, in order that women might still find husbands. Needless to say, the Salafis completely ignore the proviso of 'extraordinary circumstance' and marry more than one wife simply to have sexual relations more often.

Finally, in the Salafi *Zawaj Mu'aqqat* ('temporary marriage') a man can get married for a day or two, or even for only an hour (notwithstanding that he has to recognize any offspring by his 'former wife'). In short, the Salafis sacrifice the rights of marriage and family, and create a society full of 'cast off' women with diminished prospects of real or permanent marriage, just in order to facilitate sex relations for themselves.

19. ENFORCEMENT OF RELIGION

The Qur'an clearly states: *There is no compulsion in religion ...* (2:256). Yet somehow the Salafis manage to understand from this that not only should religion be enforced upon people, but that *their version* of it should be enforced upon people. In Saudi Arabia there are *Mutawi*s (who are sort of 'official Wahhabi enforcers') who go around the country with sticks hitting people who do not pray or who omit other things the former consider important. In Afghanistan under the Taliban there was a 'Ministry of Virtue and Vice' (connected to the Taliban Secret Intelligence) with wide-ranging powers to intrude into people's lives and homes to make sure that everyone was abiding by all of the regime's edicts.

20. DISRESPECT FOR THE SACRED; SCORN OF HISTORY, CULTURE AND HERITAGE

Because of their rejection of Islamic tradition, the Salafis have no concept of the intrinsic worth of humanity's historical, cultural and religious heritage. Their record of destruction of monuments, be they of sacred — even to Islam — historical or cultural significance is devastating. The world is well aware of the Taliban's dynamiting the unique 1700-year-old Buddhist statues in the Bamiyan province of Afghanistan in early 2001, and somewhat aware of Saudi Arabia's destruction of the unique and beautiful Ottoman fort of Ajyad outside the Ka'ba in Mecca in early 2002 to make way for another modern hotel complex. However, few people are aware that the Salafis have systematically destroyed every ancient sepulchre they have ever held power over, under pretext that praying in a sepulchre is tantamount to polytheism (even if one is praying there only to God). Thus when the Wahhabis entered the city of Jeddah in 1925 they destroyed the grand, antediluvian tomb there attributed to Eve (the word '*Jeddah*' in Arabic means 'grandmother', and the city, from time immemorial, was supposed to be where Eve died, having been cast out of the Earthly Paradise, identified with *Arabia Felix*, in the Yemen). In that same year, 1925, having conquered Medina, the Wahhabis destroyed the famous cemetery of Baqi' including the beautiful tombs there of the Prophet Muhammad's daughter Fatima and his grandson Hasan (amongst many others). They were on the point of destroying the Prophet Muhammad's own tomb, before finally being stopped by King Abd al-Aziz himself. Since then, however, they have destroyed the 1400-year-old house of the Prophet and his wife, the Lady Khadija, in Mecca to make way for a car park; they have obliterated the entire old cities of Mecca and Medina, including their walls and *souq*s; they have cut down most of the blessed mountains around Mecca and covered them with highways and crass commercial centres; they have connected the sacred well of Zamzam in Mecca to the city's modern water and sewage systems; and have laid waste countless ancient, religious, historical and cultural sites from Algeria to Yemen to Pakistan. Worst of all, perhaps they have cut down, to barely a few rocks, the sacred hills of Safa and Marwa next to the Ka'ba, even though walking between them seven times comprises an essential part of both the greater

(*Hajj*) and lesser (*'Umra*) pilgrimages, and even though the Qur'an specifically says:

> *Lo! [The hills] of Safa and Marwa are among the indications of God. It is therefore no sin for whosoever is on pilgrimage to the House [of God] or visiteth it, to go around them. And he who doeth good of his own accord, lo! God is Responsive, Aware. (2:158)*

On the other hand, the ancient pilgrim's road from Jeddah to Mecca is now studded with Vegas-style advertisement billboards declaring everything from 'Pizza Hut: Now in Mecca!' to 'The best way to kill a cockroach!'

21. DRESS (AND UNIFORMS)

We mentioned above that Wahhabi-Salafi women are forced to wear black clothes with black veils covering their faces (and even black gloves lest they should touch a man). However, the Prophet said that a woman's face or hands should not be covered, and although traditional Islam required modest dress for men and women *alike,* black was never worn in traditional Islam. On the contrary, the Prophet and his companions tried (although they were poor) to wear clothes that were colourful, noble and beautiful.

It is interesting to note that Salafi men also have a sort of unofficial uniform: it consists of a *thawb* or *dishdash* (a sort of long, thick, one-piece shirt) which, unlike other Muslims, they keep above the ankles; an Arab headgear (*hatta*) without the familiar black cord rings on the top of the head; a long, unkempt beard — although the Prophet once corrected a person for not combing his hair — without a moustache (or with only a 'stubble-length' one); flip-flops, and a few twigs (*miswaqs*) in their upper pockets which they use for brushing their teeth.

22. REJECTION OF VARIOUS
SPIRITUAL PRACTICES

The Salafis have a host of other practices that are unique to them in the history of Islam. Among these are: they permit themselves to move any number of times during the formal prayers (in the four Sunni *Madhahib* only three minor movements are allowed before having to start again); they twiddle their right index finger in a circular motion during the seated part of the formal prayer; they forbid the traditional asking of blessings upon the Prophet after the *Adhan* (call to prayer); they forbid the visiting of graves[35] to pray for individual dead (although the Prophet himself visited his daughter's grave and prayed for her, and although the Qur'an specifically mentions — in 102:1–2 — the practice of visiting graves to pray for the dead as a good 'reminder' for heedless and worldly souls); they forbid people to invoke the Divine Name (*Allah*) alone as such; they forbid people to ask for the Prophet's blessings (*Tawassul*), and so on. Most of these practices originate in misreading and misunderstanding the Qur'an and the *Hadith,* and are the cause of considerable friction between simple traditional Muslims and themselves.

On the other hand, the Salafis do insist — also because of misreading and misunderstanding the Qur'an and the *Hadith* and because of generally not seeing the wood for the trees — in the stringent possible terms on minor things like holding a glass to drink only with one's right hand. Now, Muslims handle

[35] According to the Salafis graves should not even be marked and families of the dead should not, when passing by graveyards, pray for their individual dead but for all dead Muslims, as if the eternal soul lost its individuality after death. If this were the case what would be the object of Heaven and Hell in Islam?

42

their food with their right hands and use their left hands in the bathroom as a *Sunna* convention with a profound symbolism but whose immediate purpose lies in reasons of hygiene, so that holding a glass with one's left hand can hardly be considered to be a breach of an essential tenet of faith. The Sheikh al-Albani was once asked if smoking, being now shown to be detrimental not only to the individual's health but also to that of those around him, should be considered forbidden (*haram*) in Islam. His answer was that smoking was only permitted (*mubah*) if the cigarette was held in the left hand!

SUMMARY

In summary we could say that **Wahhabi-Salafi ideology can be summed up by six major traits:** (1) it is **literalist**; (2) it is **anti-reason** and anti-philosophy; (3) it is **anti-culture** (or at least anti 'high-culture'); (4) it is anti-nomian (that is, **it refuses to accept traditional authority**); (5) it is **internally unstable** (it has no internal safety mechanisms or 'checks and balances'), and (6) it is **aggressive and repressive**. This is true of all Wahhabi-Salafism. It is a completely and radically different culture, mentality and religion than that of traditional Islam.

Wahhabi-Salafism as such is **not, however, murderous**. Despite its inherent internal instability that can perhaps lead it, in the wrong hands, to explode ideologically at any time, it does not, in its current form believe in, allow or encourage terrorism or the slaughter of innocent civilians. On the contrary **it bans these things strictly**. The only people who do believe in these things, and in fact practice them, are, by definition *Salafi-Takfiris*. They are only a small minority subset within the larger Salafi movement. They all, however, believe everything discussed above, but in addition to the above the **Salafi-Takfiris** believe in the following ideas:

SALAFI-TAKFIRIS ONLY

(1) *Takfir* (Declaring People to be Non-Muslims)

The Prophet warned: *When a man calls his brother an unbeliever, it returns [at least] to one of them.*[36] Thus, traditionally, no Muslim could call another Muslim an unbeliever (no matter what faults that person had, and no matter what sins they had committed) unless that other person had first publicly confessed to being one. This prudence was very important because apostasy was considered to be one of the most serious possible crimes and was punishable by death (although people, in this case, had to be given three chances to recant their unbelief). The Takfiris give themselves the right to declare other Muslims to be apostates (hence their name, *Takfiri*) for mere crimes (real or imaginary) or for spiritual practices with which they do not agree or that they do not understand; and of course they themselves are the judges of this! This is usually a prelude to assassinating such unfortunate people, or to calling on others to assassinate them.

Takfiris also regard all Christians and Jews as unbelievers (whereas Orthodox Muslims regard them as 'People of the Book', 'fellow believers but of the previous Scriptures'), thereby giving themselves the right to kill these too.

(2) Rejection of Political Authority

In traditional Islam Muslims are religiously bound to obey their legitimate rulers (even if these commit sins and are personally dissolute) in all matters that do not contradict the Shari'a. The Qur'an says: *O ye who believe! Obey God, and obey the messenger and those of you who are in authority...* (4:59).

Now the different *Madhahib* are not in full agreement about

---

[36] *Sahih Muslim,* 'Kitab al-Iman', n.116.

what exactly makes a ruler legitimate, but it suffices (because the *Madhahib* are all in agreement that one may *always take the easiest ruling* of any of the Orthodox *Madhahib*) that in the Hanafi *Madhhab*, a ruler is considered legitimate as long as (1) he is not a publicly-confessed apostate or heretic; (2) he upholds the public prayer; (3) he keeps public order and protects the state; and (4) he does not publicly commit or enforce a certain number of 'cardinal crimes' considered to constitute 'public sedition', *even if he does not institute the Shari'a entirely.* This is because Islam views order and the safety of the populace as the first priority of government (i.e. 'National Security'), and anarchy, sedition and civil war as the greatest danger to a nation. The Qur'an even says: *sedition is worse than [individual] killing* (2:191). The precedent for the Hanafi opinion just mentioned is that the great Caliph, 'Umar ibn al-Khattab, during a certain year of his reign when there was a famine, a heat wave and a drought, 'cancelled' the compulsory fast in Ramadan: he feared that too many people would die.

The Takfiris on the other hand, consider all political authority that does not abide by their ideas about Islam, *and all their ideas about Islam*, to be illegitimate. They consider the leaders of states where this occurs to be unlawful usurpers, so that it is permitted — or rather, *obligatory* — to kill them, and to try to take power from them.

(3) The Rules of *Jihad*

In Islam, *Jihad* (Holy War) can only be declared when Muslim lives and lands are threatened or invaded. The Qur'an says (22:39): *Sanction is given unto those who fight because they have been wronged; and God is indeed able to give them victory.* The reason for this is given as (2:251): *And if God had not repelled some men by means of others the earth would have been corrupted …*

A *Jihad* is thus a Holy War of legitimate self-defence. The Qur'an says (2:190): *And fight in the way of God those who fight you, but do not commit aggression. God loveth not the aggressors ...* However, *Jihad* can only be declared by the legitimate ruler, if and when he judges it necessary in order to protect Muslim life, limb and land. At that point it is the sacred duty of all able-bodied Muslim men in neighbouring lands to participate in the *Jihad*, and this on pain of eternal damnation. However, even in *Jihad* there are laws of conduct and warfare that may not be breached no matter what the enemy does, for 'two wrongs do not make a right'. The passage we quoted in the preface contains the summary of the rules of *Jihad* as made by the first Caliph, Abu Bakr, and is considered authoritative for all traditional Sunnis. Moreover, the Prophet himself said:

> *Attack in the Name of God, but do not revert to treachery; do not kill a child; neither kill a woman; do not wish to confront the enemy ...*[37]

Finally, the Qur'an says:

> *O ye who believe, be upright for God, witnesses in justice; and let not hatred of a people cause you to be unjust. Be just — that is closer to piety.* (5:8)

Thus there is no 'total war' in Islam; no 'scorched earth policy'; no killing of non-combatants; no bombing of civilians 'to break the enemy's will to resist' (as in Hiroshima and Nagasaki) and so on. These are all *totally alien and immoral concepts whatever the circumstances* in traditional Islam. Indeed, the historical record of traditional Muslim armies in this respect is exemplary,

[37] Al-Waqidi, *Kitab al-Maghazi*, vol.3, pp.1117–1118.

especially when contrasted with that of Christian and Crusader armies.

The Takfiris, on the other hand, neither respect the rules for declaring *Jihad*, nor the rules of conduct in *Jihad*. They kill innocent men, women and children indiscriminately and at will. One need only look at the 100,000 people slaughtered in Algeria over the last decade to comprehend the full horror of this. It is instructive to note there, moreover, that the GIA which is Takfiri, butchered (often with axes) women and children (and admitted to it), whereas the FIS, whose leaders are Salafi, killed only people who were working for the government, 'in revenge'.

(4) Suicide

In Islam, as in Christianity and Judaism before it, suicide is considered to be an unpardonable sin precisely because it closes the door to Divine Mercy. Yet the Takfiris have a secret Fatwa that states that someone who *deliberately kills himself* whilst attempting to kill enemies (as identified by them, of course) is a martyr (*Shahid*) and therefore goes straight to Heaven (as if Heaven was theirs to dispose of). This explains the *personal motivation* of individual terrorists — that is, the reward these terrorists believe they will receive for committing such acts and thus the reason why they are willing to commit them — not only in the suicide attacks on the USA on September 11th, 2001, but also in other suicide attacks including those on other Muslims (such as the one which killed Afghan Military Commander Ahmad Shah Massoud on September 9th, 2001, as will be discussed later). The Takfiris even have a Fatwa saying that someone who commits suicide rather than let himself be captured (and thereby risk giving out information to 'the enemy') is also a martyr! Finally, the Takfiris believe that since martyrdom takes one straight to Heaven — thereby erasing all human sin and consequently all Divine retribution — those with the intention of martyrdom can indulge in whatever they like by way of peccadilloes, physical pleasures and human vices before they die: thus many of the nineteen terrorists involved in the September 11th attacks spent their final weeks visiting brothels and nightclubs! All this is to say then that every Takfiri is potentially an indiscriminate human bomb and that Takfiris believe in one of the most monstrous inversions that has ever crossed the human mind: *that you can be as bad as you like, but as long as you kill people and/or yourself, you will attain ultimate salvation.*

(5) Assassination and Terrorism

Having given themselves the authority to declare people apostates; having rejected traditional political authority; having not only sanctioned suicide, but hallowed it; and having discarded all the rules of *Jihad*, it is all too easy for the Takfiris to resort to assassination and terrorism. This answers all the questions asked in the Preface about who could commit the events of September 11th, 2001, *for Bin Laden and the Qa'eda network, are precisely Takfiris.* It also answers the question of how Bin Laden could call himself a Muslim, and claim to be acting in the name of Islam, and yet have completely ignored all of Islam's rules about killing and about *Jihad*. Ultimately, the Takfiri ideology explains not just the monstrous events of September 11th, but how it is possible to admit to them and to feel righteous about them.

III

The Soil of Fundamentalism: Why Does it Take Root?

THE FERTILE SOIL

BEFORE TURNING to how the Salafis actively spread their ideas and organize themselves politically, we must first consider the social and political circumstances that predisposes many Muslims to be receptive to their ideas. If these circumstances were not present in the first place, no matter what means and stratagems the Salafis employed to spread them, they would meet with little success. Thus these factors and circumstances are the 'fertile soil' in which fundamentalism take root, and as such are extremely important to consider. Specifically they are:

Poverty and unemployment
Despite oil money the Islamic world is still one of the poorest and most under-developed swaths of the globe, and this in itself creates internal social tensions and frustrations that predispose people *a priori* to receiving any militant movement well.

Ignorance of orthodox religion
The decline of traditional Islamic education and its replacement by Western-style and largely secular education both at primary and university level in Islamic countries, combined

49

with the invasion of the Islamic world by Western-style popular culture (and in particular television) has left educated people much more ignorant of the essential substance of their religion than in former times. This in turn has left the door open for fundamentalism to come through.

Illiteracy
Conversely, much of the Islamic world is still illiterate, and illiterate popular piety, no matter how deep and how well-intentioned, lacks the arguments with which to refute fundamentalism.

Ignorance of Arabic
Only about 20 per cent of Muslims understand Arabic, and therefore 80 per cent of Muslims have no access to the sacred texts in their original language. This leaves them susceptible to being told that 'the Qur'an actually says this' or that 'the Prophet actually said that'. Since Salafism is largely an export by Arabs to other Muslims, non-Arab Muslims are inherently at a disadvantage when trying to resist it.

Discontentment due to social and political oppression
The governments of too many Islamic countries are repressive if not tyrannical. Moreover, state control and intrusion into the lives of individuals was anyway never as great over the course of Islamic history as it is in modern times. Thus many rightly feel frustrated and oppressed, and this can easily be channelled into fundamentalism, and even into suicidal terrorism.

Wounded pride
Muslims are collectively all too conscious of having been the dominant and premier civilization in the world for more or less a thousand years after the death of the Prophet. They are equally all too conscious of being nowadays politically, economically,

militarily and technologically inferior to the West, despite comprising over one fifth of the world's population. This translates into a historical sense of humiliation which is easily manipulated by the fundamentalist pedagogy.

Confusion and disequilibrium
Whether Muslims admit or not, the Islamic world (and indeed perhaps the whole world) is confused and bewildered by the pace of technological and 'lifestyle' change in the modern world. It should be borne in mind that technology has changed more during the twentieth century than it did all over the world for the previous 6,000 years, and that now every twenty-five years sees as much technological change as during the whole twentieth century. This, compounded with the often competing demands of traditional culture, creates a social and emotional disequilibrium against which the apparently simple certainties of Islamic fundamentalism can provide some relief and stability.

Palestine
Last but by no means least, there are real historical grievances that the Islamic World has to complain about at the hands of the West. However, as alluded to in the Preface, the USA, not having been an old colonial power, is not responsible for any of these, with the exception perhaps (at least in the minds of Muslims) of Palestine in the period subsequent to 1960.[38]

As regards Palestine, the following facts should be remembered: in 1900 there were 40,000 Jews in historical Palestine (that is, what is now Israel, the West Bank and Gaza) and

[38] It is extremely instructive to note that Zogby polls in the various Arab and Islamic countries over the year following September 11th, 2001 consistently show that between 65 to 80 per cent of all Arabs and Muslims harbour the issue of Palestine as their main grievance against the USA.

840,000 Arabs (exactly twenty-one times their number) and it was under Islamic control. One hundred years later, in the year 2000, there were approximately 5,500,000 Jews and 3,000,000 Arabs (including the ones with Israeli citizenship), and not only were they all under Jewish control, but the Palestinians did not have their own state anywhere whereas obviously Jews did (Israel). Now whatever the historical grievances of Jews in Europe were, the fact is that they acquired and retained the land of historical Palestine by force (admittedly against overwhelming odds), and what is more they kept it by force with the help of the West, and in particular during the years 1960–2000 with the help of the USA. Moreover, in the year 2000 there were at least 5,000,000 Palestinians, descended from the original 840,000 in 1900, living stateless and in Diaspora all over the world, whereas of the 5,500,000 Jews in Israel, 5000,000 are descended from Jews that in 1900 did not live in historical Palestine. And as for ancient historic claims, if the ancestor of the Jews (Isaac, also called *Israel*) lived in Palestine 4000 years ago, his father Abraham having come there from Ur in Iraq, then the Canaanites and the Jebusites, from whom the Palestinians are descended, lived in Palestine 6,000 years ago (see Genesis 10:15–19), and have lived there without intermission ever since.

But all of this is not even the main point in Muslim eyes, and most Muslims now accept, if not respect, the state of Israel as such. The point is Jerusalem. This city is as sacred to Muslims as it is to Jews and Christians, and if the Muslims do not get some sort of sovereignty over their own holy sites there (and consequently some state for the Palestinians), all Muslims in the world (fundamentalists and traditionalists alike) will continue to have a *grievance based on faith* against the West, and in particular the USA. (Needless to say Israel's heavy-handed behaviour in the occupied territories only exacerbates this situation.) This grievance will in turn continue to be exploited by the Islamic fundamentalists, and thus they (and the terrorists among them) will always have a sympathetic audience in the Islamic world at large.[39] If, on the other hand, the West, or the USA in particular, were to broker a peaceful settlement in Palestine, the festering sore which Palestine is would immediately turn into a healing balm.

---

[39] It is interesting to note, moreover, that every dictator that has ever come to power in a coup in the Arab World during the years 1950–2000, has done so with the name of Palestine on his lips (from Nasser to Qasim to Qaddafi to Hafez al-Assad to Saddam Hussein).

IV

The *Modus Operandi* of the Salafis: How do they Spread?

THE LEADERSHIP

T HE WAHHABI-SALAFI movement does not have an overt and clearly-defined leadership. Nevertheless it does have an effective if clandestine leadership that controls, directs, monitors and funds its global activities and gives it political cover and credibility when needed. This is not commonly admitted but is very clearly seen simply in the fact that as soon as an authoritative *Fatwa* (religious ruling or edict) emerges from their leadership, it is adopted and discussed *within 24 hours* in almost every Salafi mosque in the world. The leadership has five main hierarchical tiers. In ascending order they are:

The committed rank and file Salafis
The '*Foot-Soldiers*'; these hang about Salafi mosques wearing their Salafi uniforms (see previous chapter) waiting on their local sheikhs' every word, repeating the slogans they hear from them mindlessly, and imagining that they are being pious thereby. This tier is generally uneducated or poorly-educated and provides the 'muscle' with which the Salafis beat up their ideological opponents in mosques and universities. It also provides the 'cannon-fodder' — the 'common soldiers' — for their conflicts around the world.

The local political activists

The '*NCOs*'; these tend to be slightly more educated than the 'foot-soldiers' — often in secular affairs or through secular education — but not in religious affairs. It is they who organize rallies, distribute books, pamphlets and posters, raise money, do the accounting, and are active in local politics.

The Wahhabi-Salafi sheikhs

The '*Officers*'; these are the real local leaderships, the ones who occupy the local mosques (as imams), give the Friday sermons, teach in the local madrasas or universities or schools, and tell their followers how to run every detail of their lives. These invariably receive salaries from the Salafi 'High Command' in Saudi Arabia (or its proxies in Kuwait and Qatar) and money for almost every project they can think of, from building more mosques and schools to giving out books and distributing propaganda. Most of these sheikhs at one point or another will have studied in Saudi or Qatari universities and have imbibed the full dose of Wahhabi-Salafi ideology from those days, or will have studied under someone locally who in turn studied there. Obviously radical Salafi-Takfiri sheikhs are by definition completely 'outside' of this group, but some of them nevertheless continue to receive salaries from the 'High Command' which does not always know how far the local sheikhs have gone.

Idarat Hayat al-Buhuth wal Da'wa wal-Irshad

The '*Military High Command*'. Based in Riyadh, Saudi Arabia, the *Idarat Hayat al-Buhuth wal Da'wa wal-Irshad* (commonly known as *Hayat al-Da'wa*, the Da'wa Organization), and, secondarily its proxy, the *Jam'iyat Ihya al-Turath* of Kuwait (which is basically an outpost of the latter but with its own considerable funds), and its 'front' in Mecca, the Muslim World League

(*Rabitat al-'Alam al-Islami*) — is the Wahhabi-Salafi *'Military High Command'* and its Headquarters. Formerly headed by Bin Baz and now headed by 'Abd al-Rahman Aal al-Sheikh, this organization is the main 'funder' or organizer of Wahhabi-Salafi activities all over the world, and it is absolutely astounding how many salaries they give out, directly or indirectly, all over the world. They also fund, direct and organize the religious universities, madrasas and schools in Saudi Arabia (and in fact all over the world through the local sheikhs as mentioned). They control and fund the local *mutawis* ('religious enforcers') in Saudi Arabia formally known as the *Jama'at al-Amr bil Ma'aruf wal-Nahiy 'an al-Munkar;* they fund the Salafi publishing houses and media institutes all over the world, and they issue the ultimate religious edicts (Fatwas) for the Salafi movement. They are themselves largely funded by the Saudi Government, but not entirely any more for now they have either coerced or convinced any number of very wealthy individual Gulf businessmen to donate money to them, such that these have become an important source of income for them. Of course they also have a number of organizations which collect the *Zakat* money of ordinary people all over the world for them. Also, whilst the Saudi Government appoints their leader, Saudi Government control over them is not 100 per cent, and there are semi-independent sheikhs within their leadership that have tremendous powers. What keeps them on good terms, however, is the money which flows from Government coffers to placate them.

The Saudi Royal Family and the Aal al-Sheikh Family [40]
The *'Civilian Political Leadership'*. Whilst the Saudi Royal family and Government (these two are, at their highest levels,

[40] **The Aal al-Sheikh Family.**
The Aal al-Sheikh family are the descendents of Muhammad bin 'Abd al-Wahhab (hence the name *Aal al-Sheikh,* which means 'family of the Sheikh',

synonymous: there are no non-royals holding any independent real political power in Saudi Arabia)[41] deplore and condemn the radical Salafi-Takfiris, and hunt them down whenever and wherever they can (so that they now consider each other mortal enemies), they nevertheless support the 'World Wahhabi-Salafi Movement' as such to the hilt, financially. This occurs for six tactical reasons (despite the fact that many of the senior royals personally find the Salafis too radical and even distasteful): first, they owe their original historical legitimacy to them.[42]

---

i.e. 'Abd al-Wahhab), the eponymous founder of the Wahhabi movement. They are very much married into the Saudi Royal family and are second in prestige only to them in Saudi Arabia. This is a deliberate Saudi tactic, for they use them and their prestige amongst rank and file Wahhabis as a front through which to run the religious establishment. Indeed, the Ministry of Justice, the Ministry of Religious Affairs, the National *Mufti* and the Head of the *Da'wa* Organization (and a number of other posts such as Head of Royal Protocol) are all but hereditary in the Aal al-Sheikh Family. They are thus extremely loyal to the Saudis.

[41] The Prime Minister, the Minister of Defense, the Minister of the Interior, the Head of the National Guard, the Chief of Intelligence (and all their deputies) are all members of the Royal Family, as are the Foreign Minister, the Ambassador to the USA and all the local governors of provinces (not to mention countless lesser civilian and military posts — the Saudi Royal Family is no less than 40,000 strong). That is not to say that non-royals do not rise to high-profile technocratic jobs (e.g. the Minister of Petroleum), for they do; it is only that the holders of such posts do not make policy, but only implement it, and have no real military or political power.

[42] As already touched on, their ancestor Muhammad ibn Sa'ud (d.1765) was only a local Bedouin chieftain in the village of Dar'iyya when he met Muhammad bin 'Abd al-Wahhab in 1744, and gave him shelter, and in turn became the political leader of 'Abd al-Wahhab's ideological movement. This movement did not get very far, but 150 years later, at the turn of the twentieth century, a cast of direct descendents (including 'Abd al-Aziz bin Sa'ud, later King 'Abd al-Aziz) did, mainly by combining fanaticism with art: they defeated all their Bedouin opponents in the Najd desert of Arabia, and even swept aside 1,000 years of Hashemite (descendents of the

Second, their current form of government, whereby they do not have to deal with any real form of democracy (at least in the modern Western understanding of the term), is justified and given a mantle of legitimacy by the Wahhabi sheikhs. Third, they fear them and the trouble they can make inside the kingdom, which cannot be underestimated. Fourth, by funding them they manage to maintain some sort of control over them, and thereby often manage to moderate them. Fifth, they are a useful tool to beat back Shi'a fundamentalists, whom the former fear. This became particularly important after the Iranian Revolution of 1979, especially bearing in mind Iran's proximity to Saudi Arabia and the fact that there is a large Shi'a minority (now brutally oppressed by the Wahhabis) in Saudi Arabia, and that its neighbour Iraq has a Shi'a majority (albeit not in control of the government). Lastly, simply, they use them to extend their influence and prestige all over the Islamic World.

Thus the Saudi Royal Family has the same nervous relationship with the Wahhabi movement that a civilian government has with a restive military which is nominally under it, but which it fears, and which it cannot control except through placation and funding. In addition to funding it, moreover, they do provide two other important services to it: they give it

---

Prophet Muhammad: the name 'Hashim' being that of the Prophet's own great-grandfather the same Hashemite; that same family survives in Jordan, which they managed to hold on to from 1921) rule in the Hijaz, in 1925, to form the Kingdom of Saudi Arabia in 1932.

It must be said, however, that even King 'Abd al-Aziz, although he came to power in the name of Wahhabism, had an ambiguous relationship (to say the least) with the Wahhabi military hordes (the *Ikhwan*). In 1928 they tried to oust even him, but he defeated them at the famous battle of Sabila, and thereupon put to death a number of their more radical leaders who were responsible for wanton murder and sedition.

political cover in international bodies and arenas and the like, and they co-ordinate with friendly foreign intelligence services for it, to know when and where and how they may expand it, with the unspoken approval of these intelligence agencies. This was particularly the case in the Afghan War against the Soviets, but happened much more than is commonly admitted after September 11th, 2001.

THE MODUS OPERANDI

The Salafis have a frightening array of strategies and means by which they spread their ideology popularly all over the world wherever Muslims are to be found, and by which they establish political presence in practically every country, if not city, in the world. These include:

(1) Salaries and Stipends

As already indicated, the Wahhabi-Salafis have, in every country, a startling amount of people on their payrolls. *Every* Wahhabi or Salafi sheikh that preaches in an active mosque anywhere in the world receives in some way or another a salary or a stipend that originates from the Gulf (often in addition to, but greater than, the salary they receive locally from that mosque). Many of the 'political activists' and 'rank and file' Salafis also receive such salaries. Many local political and tribal leaders who are not even Salafi also receive these salaries, in order to buy either their silence or at least their neutrality. These salaries never come through NGOs, but either through Saudi Embassies' 'Religious' or 'Cultural Attachés' or through an unofficial 'local agent' (invariably someone trusted by his superiors in the Gulf, who goes backwards and forwards delivering monies, and making recommendations). These 'local agents' often also 'direct' those on the payroll, to make specific statements or take certain actions.

(2) *Zakat*

In countries where the Salafis are well established they raise their own funds by collecting *Zakat* (which, as explained, it is compulsory for Muslims to give, and which consists of one-fortieth of each person's income plus savings, annually) under the pretext of distributing them to the needy. This often proves quite lucrative for them, and provides a potentially limitless income for their activities.

(3) Education

This is perhaps the most effective of all the Salafis' resources and strategies. In Islamic countries there is usually an obligatory religious studies curriculum at the primary level. Some of these curriculums in the different Islamic countries are either written by the Salafis, and if not written by them, are certainly influenced by them and contain their ideas. At the university level their influence is even greater, with many university syllabuses and reading lists composed entirely of their books even in a completely skewered way. As soon as a Salafi penetrates into any educational system this is the first thing he tries to do, and as there are now thousands of Salafi teachers and professors in every educational system in the world (even in countries that are not sympathetic to Salafism), most Islamic studies' curriculum and reading lists have by now been compromised. Moreover, as soon as Salafis entrench themselves in a university they oppose, refuse to employ or promote, fail, and belittle anyone not holding their views, be it student or teacher.

They also directly control an untold number of schools, *madrasas* (religious schools) and universities (or at least their departments of religion), and provide thousands of research grants and scholarships every year to students (natives and 'promising' foreigners alike) who agree to study in these. This occurs not just in countries which are openly Salafi (e.g. Saudi Arabia, Qatar, Afghanistan when it was ruled by the Taliban) but in practically every country in the world including the USA. Particularly worrying are the Salafi madrasas which have sprung up by the thousands in the years 1981–2001 in South Asia (notably Afghanistan, Pakistan, India, Bangladesh, Malaysia and Indonesia) with Saudi financing, Pakistani logistical support and Western silence, because these countries contain over 550 million Muslims, the vast majority of whom are poor, frustrated and uneducated. If unchecked this is a time bomb waiting to explode.

(4) Media

The Salafis control or influence an impressive global network of newspapers, journals, radio stations, television and news stations (many satellite) and now even film studios. They harness these to their cause, using them to spread if not their views, views inherently sympathetic to their ideology. Above all they use the above to subtly portray the idea — to Muslims and to the West alike — that Salafi Islam is mainstream Islam. Also, the Salafis put a lot of money into making attractive, subsidized films and television programs which vilify their enemies (such as the Sufis) and glorifying their heroes (such as Ibn Taymiyya), and it must be said that Arab and Islamic television networks air these indiscriminately over and over again. In other words, they successfully mobilize modern media institutions and propaganda instruments to their own ends.

(5) Information (and Misinformation)

Equally, they own or influence a large number of important publishing houses, internet sites, libraries, bookshops, 'research institutes' and 'think tanks' all over the globe. They use these to publish their own books, posters and magazines (written by their 'approved' sheikhs, and translated in every country into the local languages) — all of the finest quality printing — and distribute them all over the world free of charge. An Arab proverb says that a person is 'owned' by the books he reads, and in this day and age when people read so few books, this is particularly true. Thus giving out free quality-print books is an especially effective tactic for 'hooking' people, especially young students who are more easily influenced, have not yet read much, and who anyway cannot afford to buy anything else. They also make their own promotional posters, banners, videotapes and cassettes (these last two being particularly widespread and popular) and hand them out free all over the world, and these are very effective among illiterate people, or among people either too lazy or too busy to read. These tapes contain everything from their sheikhs' sermons, to images of women available for 'temporary marriages', and even images of 'Salafi warriors' butchering enemies in what they call *Jihad*. Finally, it should be noted that in countries they control the Salafis censure and ban any books attacking their beliefs or challenging their ideas, and even make it illegal to possess them.

As for misinformation it hardly need be said that much of the information put about by the Salafis is (deliberately) completely untrue — particularly with regard to historical facts — and that in addition to an aggressive 'international information campaign', they have a virulent 'international misinformation campaign', using all the means described above. This latter campaign comprises everything from simple political 'spin', to smearing and defaming the honour and characters of living individuals who disagree with them, to misrepresenting the views of others, to outright historical 'whoppers'. For example, one of their most bandied historical lies is that Sufis are feckless cowards who have never fought *Jihad* and therefore are not real Muslims.[43] Equally, they spread the rumour that the Shi'a believe that God should have given the Revelation to the Caliph Ali and not the Prophet, or that the Shi'a as such believe that the Archangel Gabriel (the bearer of Revelation) made a mistake in delivering the Revelation. This sort of 'religious' and 'historical' slander is remarkably effective and divisive among the lesser-educated Sunni masses, even in the Information Age.

(6) Mosques

This too is an extremely important tool, because every Muslim male is required at least once a week (on Fridays) to attend a communal prayer and listen to a sermon in a mosque, this being the main form of religious instruction and community contact for ordinary Muslims. Thus by controlling these institutes, which they do by the thousands all over the world, they have a captive audience for their indoctrination. Moreover, mosques traditionally provide extra religious lessons to local children throughout the week and intensively during the holy month of Ramadan. Finally, it should be noted that Saudi Arabia never builds a new mosque anywhere without stipulating that its *Imam* (preacher) be one of their sheikhs. In this way they have managed to ensconce their preachers everywhere indefinitely.

(7) Orphanages

The Salafis have an impressive portfolio of orphanages that they pay for and run all over the Islamic world. The *Hayat*

---

[43] In fact, although Sufis have never fought offensive wars and are generally apolitical, it was they who took the lead in every legitimate defensive war of resistance to colonialism in the nineteenth and twentieth centuries, earning, tellingly, even the respect of their former enemies (for the principled way they behaved during the conflict). The great resistance leaders such as Imam Shamil in the Caucasus, Emir Abd al-Qadir al-Jazairi of Algeria, Omar Mukhtar of Libya, Uthman Dan Fodio of West Africa and Ahmad Shah Massoud of Afghanistan (amongst many others) were all Sufis.

al-Ighata al-Islamiyya al-'Alamiyya (which belongs to the Mec-
can-based *Rabita al-Islamiyya* or Muslim World League) alone
has offices and orphanages in fifty-one countries all over the
world. Even in a small country like Jordan this organization
has an annual budget of around US$3 million, with 10,000
orphans in its care. Whilst local governments are understand-
ably very grateful for social assistance of this sort (the Qur'an
is particularly insistent upon the care and proper treatment of
orphans — see 107:2), this remains a mixed blessing because
the orphans invariably grow up as indoctrinated Salafis. Moreover, it need hardly be said that orphans, having no families to
tell them otherwise and being grateful to their benefactors, are
particularly vulnerable to indoctrination of any kind.

(8) **Other 'Charitable' Activities**
There are a number of other 'charitable activities' in which
the Salafis engage, largely funded by *Zakat,* all calculated to win
them sympathy and gratitude. These include feeding the poor
and providing housing for the poor and temporary shelter for
wayfarers and even refugees. It is interesting to note that the
Salafis are not yet, however, widely known — unlike the Muslim
Brotherhood — for 'Islamic Hospitals', 'Islamic Banks' or
'Islamic Emergency Aid Agencies' (notwithstanding the OIC's
Islamic Development Fund, as mentioned earlier).

(9) **Sovereign Political Power**
There are a number of Islamic countries whose governments
are officially, or semi-officially, Wahhabi or Salafi (namely Saudi
Arabia, Qatar and Afghanistan (when it was ruled by the Taliban, 1996–2001); since 1980 Pakistan has also been sympathetic), and these obviously provide them with enormous political support. They also scare other Muslims countries into not
objecting to Wahhabi-Salafi activities.

(10) **Violence, Bullying, Intimidation (and Murder)**

In every one of their mosques, and every academic institute where their control is not yet complete, Wahhabis have thugs (who are well organized, and encouraged to study martial arts), from their rank and file followers, whose mission it is to assault and batter anyone who challenges their sheikhs, argues with them or embarrasses them on points of doctrine. Their particular victims are Sufi sheikhs, whom they regard as their main competitors for popular affection, because of the generally charismatic nature and methods of these latter. In many countries (e.g. Egypt, India, Jordan) they actually organize excursions into Sufi mosques where they attack and beat up Sufi followers. Unfortunately, few Islamic countries do anything to stop this, so that in the end many opponents of the Wahhabis wind up being intimidated by them and therefore on the defensive or silent. In places like Chechnya in the mid-1990s, where there was little effective government control, the Salafis (or rather, perhaps, the Takfiris) even had **a deliberate and systematic murder and liquidation campaign** of Sufi Sheikhs so that the local Islamic 'leadership' would become theirs alone.

Recently, Salafi thuggery has 'gone cyber': the Salafis now employ computer and internet specialists to attack, crash, and 'spike' with 'viruses' the websites of their orthodox Muslim opponents (although they never, interestingly enough, attack anti-Islamic websites as such or even hard-core pornography websites). Their strategy is to keep doing this, from bases in countries like Saudi Arabia which will protect them, until (bearing in mind their superior financial resources) it becomes too expensive and too tiring to oppose them on the web, so that eventually every word written on Islam on the internet is written by them. Bearing in mind the world's (and in particular, the West's) increasing dependence on the internet as a tool for research and information, this bodes ominously.

(11) Sex
This is their most surprising tool of all, but one of their most rewarding. Because, as mentioned, they remove the constraints and safeguards around marriage, they are able to organize 'temporary marriages' (*Zawaj Mu'aqqat*) and 'marriages without dowries or rights' (*Zawaj Misyar*) amongst their followers. Indeed, they now have networks whereby they do this (often completely secretly) with the greatest of propriety, much to the delight of their followers male and female, who indulge almost in bath-house style sex and yet manage to feel virtuous about it! Needless to say, this is merely organized and sanctioned prostitution, and corrodes the fabric of traditional Islamic society through its most important institute, the family. More alarming than this is their practice of kidnapping poor and destitute non-Muslim (and sometimes merely non-Salafi) women (particularly in impoverished countries or countries where there is armed conflict) and, under the pretext that these women are prisoners-of-war (or rather *Jihad*) and therefore their slave-girls, forcing them to have sex with their followers. These shocking practices have not been well-studied by the West, because they have been kept so secret, but their details are bound to emerge sooner or later.

(12) Hijacking Legitimate Causes
Muslims are oppressed in a number of areas around the world and so have, whether it is commonly acknowledged or not, a number of legitimate causes and grievances. The Salafis try to hijack these causes (often *after* they have already been settled) thereby gaining broad Islamic popular support, raising their profile and improving their image. What is so insidious about

this tactic is that it most harms the very people they claim to be trying to support (to say nothing of the image of these in the West). Thus the Chechen people, after having essentially won the First Chechen War (1991-1995) under Dudaev, were dragged into another war by Salafi elements (e.g. Khattab)[44] who as just mentioned, had liquidated Sufi opposition to them, which this time they lost, and in which the country was all but destroyed and their hard-fought right to autonomy completely revoked! Indeed, the Taliban themselves are the result of the hijacking of a legitimate cause (the Afghan War for liberation from the Soviets), and indeed the Salafis have tried (and still are trying) to hijack every Muslim cause or grievance from Aceh and Ambon, to Bosnia and Kosovo, to Kashmir, to Mindanao.[45] It is also significant that Usama bin Laden, in his first televised statement after September 11th, 2001, tried to link the events of that day to not only the US military presence in Saudi Arabia, but also to the situation in Palestine and the sanctions on Iraq.

(13) Fatwas

As mentioned earlier, the Salafis ignore the traditional checks and preconditions for issuing a *Fatwa* or religious decree. Consequently, the Salafi leadership has the laxest 'rent-a-Fatwa' system in Islamic history. They can get edicts for whatever cause

---

[44] Khattab was finally reported killed by the Russian military on April 25th, 2002.

[45] The situation in Mindanao represents another potential tragedy because the MNLF (Moro National Liberation Front) had reached a seemingly equitable agreement for autonomy with the Philippine Government in 1996 and had demobilised, and the MILF (Moro Islamic Liberation Front) were on the point of demobilising themselves, when (in 2002) they were almost dragged back into a conflict scenario by the Takfiri group Abu Sayyaf. On the other hand the Free Aceh Movement in Indonesia has (at least publicly) stoutly resisted any usurpation by foreign elements.

they want, without paying too much attention to what the Islamic sacred texts *actually say* and to what Muslims have actually agreed upon throughout Islamic history. This may initially seem to be a positive development (as it helps the leadership be more practical) but in fact the contrary is true, for it is a two-edged sword: every moderate Fatwa made by a Salafi sheikh immediately discredits that sheikh for ever (and the leadership has to then spend years and millions grooming, establishing and 'marketing' a successor), and for every moderate Fatwa organized by the Saudi leadership (with the greatest effort, and they are obviously not always that moderate) there are one hundred extremist Fatwas not made by the leadership but rather by the 'officer-class' sheikhs. An example of this is Usama bin Laden's 1998 Fatwa (see Appendix I): this so-called 'Fatwa' has no basis whatsoever in Islamic jurisprudence, scripture or tradition; it quotes the Qur'an completely out of context; it misrepresents the political facts, and it perverts logic, in order to call upon all Muslims to attack and kill all US citizens everywhere they can (without differentiating between military targets and civilian targets, and without sparing women, children, the elderly, or the disabled). In other words, the gratuitous issuing of Fatwas is an evil Pandora's box opened by the Salafis, and one that gives no hope to anyone but them. Rather, it perversely gives the illusion of propriety and Islamic sanction to the nastiest and most immoral ideas imaginable. Finally, it should be said that traditional Islam, whilst obviously not a religion based on passivity and complacence, and whilst obviously a religion born into a different culture and mindset than the modern West, is inherently flexible and encourages reason, moderation and compassion in all things. The Prophet said: *Religion is to be easy ... Do not be extremists.*[46]

[46] *Sahih Bukhari*, 'Kitab al-Iman', ch.29.

(14) *Hajj* and *Umra* (Islamic Pilgrimage)

The Wahhabi-Salafis use the *Hajj* and the *Umra* as an opportunity to propagate their ideas and doctrines: millions of people come to the holy places every year and the Salafis use their control of Mecca and Medina to inculcate their practices and doctrines into these pilgrims: through sermons, free pamphlets, teaching their customs and above all through using the fact that they control the holy places to pretend that their version of Islam is the correct and original one. Also the Salafis give away 'pilgrimage-permits' to enter Saudi Arabia ('pilgrimage-permits' to Saudi Arabia are restricted by quota and country because there are many more Muslims wanting to go on pilgrimage than there is room to accommodate them) which the Saudi government and religious establishment give 'under the table' to reward their followers all over the world, and to create new ones. This is effective because, as mentioned earlier, it is religiously compulsory for every Muslim adult with means to make the pilgrimage at least once in his/her life.

(15) Alliances and Trojan Horses

In many Islamic countries where they are still weak the Salafis have proved very adept at making local alliances in order to infiltrate larger local Islamic parties and groups, thereby gaining access to their resources and popular credibility, and infecting them with their doctrines, and, ultimately, gaining control of them completely. This 'Trojan Horse' or 'virus' strategy saves them the trouble of rivalry with existing Islamic groups; gives them a 'cover' and a (concealing) image; gives them an already-established local influence, and spares them the work of setting up new 'Islamic institutes'. Particular dupes of this shrewd thinking are the puritanical, reformist Deobandi movement of the Indian Subcontinent (who now seem to have entirely dove-tailed with the Salafis) and the Muslim Brotherhood, who, as we have discussed, are inherently pre-disposed to *de facto* adopt Salafi positions because of their cardinal rule of 'avoiding (inter-Islamic) controversies'.[47] Indeed, many of the Muslim

---

47 **The Jama'at-ul-Tabligh.**
The other great dupes of the Salafi 'virus' strategy — albeit to a lesser extent than the Muslim Brotherhood — are the *Jama'a* (group) of *Tabligh* (conveyance, transmission — of the Message of Islam). The Tabligh Movement was started in 1926 near Delhi, India by Sheikh Muhammad Ilyas Khandalawi (1885–1944). It was then for a long time headed by his son Sheikh Muhammad Yusuf Khandalawi, and in 1947 its centre moved to Pakistan because of the Partition of India. Muhammad Ilyas came from a Sufi family and started the movement as a reaction to Hindu proselytizing amongst Muslims. The movement consisted of (and consists of) 'itinerant preaching': that is, of Muslims going out systematically, in small, organized groups all over the world (for periods of three days, 40 days, 4 months or even 1 year) and preaching to any Muslims who will listen to them according to 'the six principles of Tabligh'. These principles are (1) *Kalima* (teaching the testimony of faith of Islam, as described in Chapter 1); (2) *Salat* (teaching the five daily ritual prayers); (3) *Dhikr* (teaching the basic doctrines of Islam, as laid out by another member of the Khandalawi family, Sheikh Muhammad Zakariyya Khandalawi, in his book *Tablighi Nisab*); (4) *Ikram il-Muslimin* (teaching and practicing respect for fellow Muslims); (5) *Niyya* (being sincere in religion), and (6) *Khuruj fi sabil Allah* (getting more people to go out on 'itinerant preaching', and thus creating a 'knock-on' effect for the Tablighi Movement). In principle the Tablighi agenda is completely de-politicized, extremely simple (hence its success — its annual conferences in Pakistan and Bangladesh draw about a million people from all over the world) and harmless enough, albeit that the Tablighis look fairly alarming as they scour, in packs, every city in the world (and indeed some many rural areas) in their (recommended) Indian subcontinent dress, looking for people to preach to (in the West they use the Yellow Pages to find local Muslim names), and camping out in the local mosques! However, recently many of its 'group-leader' preachers have begun to imbibe (and in turn, teach) Salafi ideology, hence creating a massive and international grass-roots Salafi propaganda machine.
One final note: the Tablighis are often (mistakenly) called *Jama'at al-Da'wa*, but should not be confused with the *Idarat al-Da'wa* of Saudi Arabia, as discussed earlier.

Brotherhood's national parties are now ideologically mostly or completely Salafi so that it is only a matter of time before these surrender local control of their parties to hard-core Salafi sheikhs. This is fully the case with the *Islah* (reform) parties of Kuwait and Yemen, and increasingly so in the cases of the Muslim Brotherhood in Jordan and the Hamas parties in Palestine and Algeria.

(16) Political Movements and Parties

In Islamic countries where it is permitted and/or expedient the Salafis form legal parties to advance their cause, or as a legal front for their political and religious activities. This, however, is only a temporary tactic to achieve power, and they neither believe in nor respect the multi-party system as such. Indeed as soon as they feel they are strong enough to fight by other means they do so. Typical examples of this are the FIS in Algeria and Gulbaldin Hekmatyar's Hizb i-Islami in pre-Taliban Afghanistan; both immediately turned to violence the moment their political ambitions were not met.

(17) 'Expats'

On any given year there are at least 5 million expatriates in Saudi Arabia alone (to say nothing of the rest of the Gulf). The majority of these come from other Islamic countries, and do financially quite well in Arabia (or at least better than they would have in their own, financially poorer, countries, which is the reason why they go there in the first place). They thus become attached to it, and impressed by it, and often come to adopt its customs, taking them back home with them when they finally leave. These people and their children (many of whom will have grown up and gone to school in Arabia) thus tend to become *de facto* ambassadors in their home countries for Salafism and Salafi ways. To appreciate the extent of this one need only walk down the street in the capitals of Islamic world from Nigeria to Egypt to Indonesia and see how many native women are covered from tip to toe in black (faces included, and often even wearing gloves) *Salafi-style:* these, more usually than not, will have had a personal contact with Saudi Arabia.

(18) Proselytizing
Last but not least there is the simple old-fashioned proselytizing. The Qur'an has a number of verses (e.g. 5:67; 16:125; 41:33) that enjoin the (above all tactful and courteous) dissemination of Islamic ideas. *All* committed Salafis (whatever their 'class') take these verses as a blanket endorsement of aggressive proselytizing, not to Islam as such, but to Salafism. Thus, in addition to a few international Salafi organizations created specifically for the purpose of proselytizing (and to many local or national ones — and perhaps to the Tablighi Movement as just mentioned), every committed Salafi must be regarded as (and indeed, acts as, given half a chance) an active Salafi proselytizer.

SALAFI-TAKFIRIS ONLY

(1) Terrorist Groups and Cells
A detailed study of all of these would require a separate study; it suffices here to note the following: (1) that ordinary Salafis do not usually participate in terrorist movements or cells (or even believe in them), and that they are usually comprised of only *Salafi-Takfiris.* (2) That the more organized among them can consist of a number of distinct 'wings' or 'elements' (such as leadership; finance; military and training; the religious and ideological wing; logistics and supplies; media and publicity; intelligence and information) often with the classic 'cell structures' such that very few people have any idea of what they are really doing. (3) That there are so many different splinter groups

and individual radicals that it is difficult to keep track of them all, especially in the Islamic countries where they breed. The best known of these groups are of course Usama bin Laden's al-Qa'eda, Ayman Zawahiri's (Egyptian) Islamic Jihad, the Algerian GIA (*Groupe Islamique Armé*), the Abu Sayyaf of the Philippines, and perhaps the Jama'a of Migbil bin Hadi al-Wadi in the Yemen.

(2) The International, Travelling Salafi Army

It is estimated that at any given moment in time since 1989 (the end of the Soviet occupation of Afghanistan) there are no less than around 20,000 trained Salafi professional soldiers and warriors worldwide who go from conflict to conflict fighting for Salafi causes around the world (e.g. Bosnia, Kosovo, Kashmir, Chechnya, Somalia) as a way of life. These tend to come from the young men of the 'Salafi foot-soldier' class but also include many rich young Salafis (who bring with them their financial resources). Having seen videos or heard news of the treatment of Muslims in X or Y place, they become outraged and pack up individually and make their way (with the help of various Salafi or Takfiri organizations) to fight in what they believe is their duty (of *Jihad*) in conflict zones. As the years go by, those who survive become hardened by local military training and/or actual conflict, and come to adopt all the Takfiri doctrines (the various Takfiri organizations also often give them salaries). Moreover, conflict becomes all they know, so that when it is over in one place they export it to another. Finally, because they come from different nationalities (in practice mostly Arabs, Pakistanis/Kashmiris, Chechens) they can always go home (when the pressure is too great) and melt into the civilian population for a while only to take up arms again later. Many of these individuals had, until 2001, coalesced into distinct military brigades connected to Usama bin Laden's al-Qa'eda, in

Taliban-controlled Afghanistan, and those not destroyed in the conflict there with the USA are sure to re-emerge in the future in other battle zones.

SUMMARY

In summary we can say that the Salafis are extremely well-funded and organized, and have used every conceivable instrument or institute (ancient and modern) and every conceivable motive (religiously, worldly or even criminal) to spread all over the world. There are no movements in the world more adept at spreading than them, and although they influence tens of millions, it is a testament to traditional Islam's genuine cultural and spiritual power — and actually to the Salafi's own innate impoverishment in these respects — that they have not reached more, despite traditional Islam's relative passivity before them. However, they are making gains, and look set, through the methods delineated above, to keep doing so, unless an international concerted effort is made to stop them.

V

Conclusion: The Danger of Salafi Ideology

SALAFISM IS NOT ORTHODOX ISLAM

A s DISCUSSED at length Salafism is a recent innovation that is completely different in form, content and above all ethical behaviour than traditional orthodox Islam. Indeed, the two have very little in common and agree on so little that many Muslims who are aware of these differences have, for a long time, been predicting that sooner or later, as Salafism grows in strength, the Salafis would wage war on traditional Muslims.[48]

[48] It is interesting to note that the legendary Ahmad Shah Massoud, the greatest Afghan military commander in the War of Liberation against the Soviets (1979–1989), viewed his continued resistance to the Taliban from 1996–2001 not as a struggle for dominance between Pashtuns on the one hand and Tajiks/Uzbeks/Shi'a Hazaris on the other hand (as the Taliban's Pakistani backers liked to depict to the Western media), but rather as a struggle between Traditional Orthodox Islam and Salafi Fundamentalism! For Massoud was, if not a Sufi of the Naqshbandi order, certainly deeply steeped in Naqshbandi tradition and views (in fact a great student of the Sufi poetry of Rumi and Hafez), and one need only examine his publicly-stated positions on issues such as the laws of *Jihad,* education, the rights of women, Islamic democracy (*Shura*), and the practices and doctrines of the Taliban, to appreciate this (see for example his 'unofficial website' at geocities.com entitled 'The Man who withstood the Red Army and Slapped Islamic Fundamentalism in the Face'). This and his personal nobility (as epitomized by his declining the Afghan Presidency in 1992) was precisely

The 'war' that the Takfiris have waged on the West is just a prelude to this larger war, as many of them, including Usama bin Laden himself, have said. Of course, they do not usually call it a 'war' but rather 'a movement to purify religion from error and heresy', using in fact almost the same words as did the Spanish Inquisition at the end of the fifteenth century.

THERE ARE 'GOOD' SALAFIS BUT THERE IS NO 'GOOD' SALAFISM

Most simple people who are religious do not usually make the effort to be so because they are bad at heart, but rather because they are good at heart, and wish to be even better. This is true too of the majority of Salafis, and of the majority of people that are influenced by them, which as we have said, number around 10 per cent of Sunni Islam (and therefore at over 100 million people all over the world). Thus it would be monstrous to say that Salafis *as such* are a 'bad element'. Nevertheless, it is hardly being judgmental to say that *the Salafi ideology* is not a positive element as regards how it encourages men to be and act, especially when contrasted with traditional Islam. Of course, it is always a tricky business to start judging good and bad from one cultural perspective (and therefore prejudice) and not another, but one cannot go far wrong with *Love the Lord thy God with all thy heart* and *Love thy neighbour as thyself* as a basic universal double touchstone for religions. According to this double touchstone it is difficult to ascertain what good Salafism, as a new ideology, fosters, particularly when compared with Orthodox Islam: it is true that it brings faith, and therefore comfort, to

---

why he was so dangerous to the Taliban, and thus why Bin Laden had to murder him on September 9th, two days before the terrorist attacks against the United States.

millions of people, but it is even more true that Islam has always done that, and in a much more tolerant, inclusive and intelligent way. For Salafism is a reduction of Islam, and one that refocuses the religion on politics and on militancy rather than on God. And it is an inherently unstable one that contains no internal doctrinal safeguards so that at any time, in the wrong hands, it may suddenly relapse to Takfiri ideology and thereby start encouraging indiscriminate assassination and terrorism, all in the name of religion. Thus it must in fairness be concluded that whilst the majority of Salafis are simple people with good intentions, the ideology of Salafism is not one that brings out this goodness, and is one that can inherently lead to 'Takfirism'.

SALAFI IDEOLOGY IS DANGEROUS AND STOPPING TERRORISM NECESSITATES FIRST CHECKING SALAFISM

Having examined Takfiri beliefs and practices it is all too obvious that not only are they the source of — and license for — indiscriminate terrorism and slaughter of Muslims and non-Muslims alike, but that terrorism and murder will not stop as long as Takfiris are around. It is also obvious that these Takfiris would love to be able to ignite a larger conflict between the Islamic world and the West, thereby perhaps provoking a World War with unforeseeable, and possibly nuclear, consequences. Then, it is no less obvious that fighting the Takfiri terrorist after he has already become one, as Western intelligence agencies have traditionally done, is like fighting the mythical hydra: every time one head is lopped off, two more immediately spring up in its place (partly because of the sympathy the very act of fighting them creates). Finally, it is obvious that the spread of Salafism as such contributes to the increase of Takfirism, for

Salafism is the ideological parent, root and base of Takfirism, even if that parent does not always support everything its child does.

Thus if 'terrorism in the name of Islam' is to be fought with any measure of success this must be done on **four simultaneous levels**: (1) the **intelligence/military level**; (2) the **political/diplomatic level**; (3) the **financial level**; and (4) the **ideological level**. The first level is obvious; it is what we have just discussed as being 'the traditional approach' of intelligence agencies, the events of September 11th proving its limitations all too well. The second and third levels are also clear: it is what the USA and its allies started to do *after* September 11th: putting political and diplomatic pressure on every country in the world to: (A) not harbour or tolerate terrorists or terrorist organizations and (B) actively cut off terrorist financial resources. Thus the fourth level, the ideological level, must be activated.[49] This means that the growth of Salafi ideology must be

---

[49] Perhaps the reason why this has never been done before is that Western intelligence agencies, despite a formidable array of high-tech and electronic intelligence-gathering methods, and despite their expertise at psychological profiling and at tracking suspects, have, nevertheless, by and large shifted away from 'human intelligence', and anyway do not usually think to delve into the subtleties of Islamic jurisprudence and theology. Moreover, even when Western intelligence agencies (and media) turn for advice to Western 'think-tanks' or academia, these are not usually sufficiently knowledgeable on the intricacies of Islamic thought to give beneficial opinions or information, partly because 'Islamic ideologies' and their implications are so vast and complex (native Muslim scholars themselves — these usually being the finest minds, with near photographic memories, recruited from the vast population of the entire Islamic World — traditionally spend their whole lives studying the religious sciences before being considered learned), and partly because Western academia has largely 'compartmentalized' knowledge into distinct academic disciplines (and taught Westerners to think that way), so that to have a full grasp of the Islamic Sciences requires not only a polymath with a photographic memory, but an expert linguist as well.

checked and contained—and its more moderate sympathizers 'reeled back' towards traditional Islam—lest more and more Muslims become Salafis and lest more and more Salafis become Takfiris. Equally, it means that Takfiri ideology itself must be eradicated.

HOW TO CHECK SALAFISM AND STOP 'TAKFIRISM'

Takfiri ideology can be tackled directly in the Islamic world: there is not much sympathy for it *as such*, for it is still universally regarded as too radical. However, any attempt to check Salafism directly or publicly by non-Muslims or by a Western government is bound not only to fail but to backfire and increase their general popular standing wildly in the Islamic world. What the West can do, however, is (A) work to **remove the factors that give rise to 'the fertile soil of fundamentalism'** as described in Chapter 3, **in particular by bringing closure to the issue of Palestine**, and by helping the poorer Islamic countries develop their economies. Western countries can also (B) put pressure on Saudi Arabia and its proxies to **stop the flow of funds to the Salafis**; ideally, they would (C) **prevent the Salafis from enacting their stratagems of propagation and expansion** as described in Chapter 4. Finally, Western countries can (D) **support 'traditional Islamic' countries** and their governments — with backing when necessary—in not only cutting off Salafi stratagems of propagation and expansion as described in Chapter 4, but also **in actively combating the spread of Salafi ideas,** as identified in Chapter 2. *In short, Salafism can be contained by an indirect attack on its causes, resources and ideas, in conjunction with a policy to support traditional Islam in its opposition to it.*

APPENDIX I

Usama Bin Laden's 1998 Fatwa on Killing American Citizens

JIHAD AGAINST JEWS AND CRUSADERS
WORLD ISLAMIC FRONT STATEMENT
February 23rd, 1998

By
Sheikh Usama bin Muhammad bin Laden
Ayman al-Zawahiri
Amir of the Jihad Group in Egypt
Abu Yasir Rifa'i Ahmad Taha
Egyptian Islamic Group
Sheikh Mir Hamzah
Secretary of the Jamiat-ul-Ulema-e-Pakistan
Fazlur Rahman
Amir of the Jihad Movement in Bangladesh

Praise be to God, who revealed the Book, controls the clouds, defeats factionalism, and says in His Book: *But when the forbidden months are past, then fight and slay the pagans wherever ye find them, seize them, beleaguer them, and lie in wait for them in every stratagem (of war);* and peace be upon our Prophet, Muhammad bin 'Abdallah, who said: 'I have been sent with the sword between my hands to ensure that no one but God is worshipped. God, who put my livelihood under the shadow of my spear, and who inflicts humiliation and scorn on those who disobey my orders.'

The Arabian Peninsula has never — since God made it flat, created its desert, and encircled it with seas — been stormed by any forces like the crusader armies, spreading in it like locusts, eating its riches and wiping out its plantations. All this is happening at a time in which nations are attacking Muslims like people fighting over a plate of food. In the light of the grave situation and the lack of support, we and you are obliged to discuss current events, and we should all agree on how to settle the matter.

No one argues today about three facts that are known to everyone; we will list them, in order to remind everyone.

First, for over seven years the United States has been occupying the lands of Islam in the holiest of places, the Arabian Peninsula, plundering its riches, dictating to its rulers, humiliating its people, terrorizing its neighbours, and turning its bases in the Peninsula into a spearhead through which to fight the neighbouring Muslim peoples. If some people have in the past argued about the fact of the occupation, all the people of the Peninsula have now acknowledged it. The best proof of this is the Americans' continuing aggression against the Iraqi people using the Peninsula as a staging post, even though all its rulers are against their territories being used to that end; but they are helpless.

Second, despite the great devastation inflicted on the Iraqi people by the crusader-Zionist alliance, and despite the huge number of those killed, which has exceeded one million — despite all this, the Americans are once again trying to repeat the horrific massacres, as though they are not content with the protracted blockade imposed after the ferocious war, or the fragmentation and devastation. So they come here to annihilate what is left of this people and to humiliate their Muslim neighbours.

Third, if the Americans' aims behind these wars are religious and economic, the aim is also to serve the Jews' petty state and divert attention from its occupation of Jerusalem and murder of Muslims there. The best proof of this is their eagerness to destroy Iraq, the strongest neighbouring Arab state, and their endeavour to fragment all the states of the region such as Iraq, Saudi Arabia, Egypt, and Sudan [and turn them] into paper statelets, and, through their disunion and weakness, to guarantee Israel's survival and the continuation of the brutal crusade occupation of the Peninsula.

All these crimes and sins committed by the Americans are a clear declaration of war on God, his Messenger, and Muslims. And *'ulama* have throughout Islamic history unanimously agreed that the *Jihad* is an individual duty if the enemy destroys the Muslim countries. This was revealed by Imam Ibn Qudama in [his book] *al-Mughni;* Imam al-Kisa'i in *al-Bada'i,* al-Qurtubi in his *Tafsir,* and the Sheikh al-Islam [Ibn Taymiyya] in his books, where he said: 'As for the fighting to repulse [an enemy], it is aimed at defending sanctity and religion, and it is a duty as agreed upon [by the *'ulama*]. Nothing is more sacred than belief except repulsing an enemy who is attacking religion and life'.

On that basis, and in compliance with God's order, we issue the following Fatwa to all Muslims:

The ruling to kill the Americans and their allies — civilians and military — is an individual duty for every Muslim who can do it in any country in which it is possible to do it, in order to liberate the al-Aqsa Mosque and the holy mosque [Mecca] from their grip, and in order for their armies to move out of all the lands of Islam, defeated and unable to threaten any Muslim. This is in accordance with the words of Almighty God, *and fight the pagans all together as they fight you all together*, and *fight them until there is no more tumult or oppression, and there prevail justice and faith in God.* This is in addition to the words of Almighty God: *And why should ye not fight in the cause of God and of those who, being weak, are ill-treated (and oppressed)? — women and children, whose cry is: 'Our Lord, rescue us from this town, whose people are oppressors; and raise for us from Thee one who will help!'*

We — with God's help — call on every Muslim who believes in God and wishes to be rewarded to **comply with God's order to kill the Americans and plunder their money wherever and whenever they find it.** We also call on Muslim *'ulama,* leaders, youths, and soldiers to launch the raid on Satan's US troops and the devil's supporters allying with them, and to displace those who are behind them so that they may learn a lesson. Almighty God said: *O ye who believe, give your response to God and His Apostle, when He calleth you to that which will give you life. And know that God cometh between a man and his heart, and that it is He to whom ye shall all be gathered.* Almighty God also says: *O ye who believe, what is the matter with you, that when ye are asked to go forth in the cause of God, ye cling so heavily to the earth! Do ye prefer the life of this world to the hereafter? But little is the comfort of this life, as compared with the hereafter. Unless ye go forth, He will punish you with a grievous penalty, and put others in your place; but Him ye would not harm in the least. For God hath power over all things.* Almighty God also says: *So lose not heart, nor fall into despair. For ye are bound to gain mastery if ye are true in faith.*

Ancient Prophecies of Fundamentalism and Religious Decline: An Unlikely but Potent Potential Vaccine

IT IS INTERESTING to note that the rise of fundamentalism and the descent of Islam into literalism after a long period of time is an ill clearly foretold in Islamic literature. The Prophet had said:

> The best of my people are my generation; then they that come after them; then they that come after them.[50]

And:

> No time cometh upon you but it is followed by a worse.[51]

And:

> Islam began as a stranger and will become once more a stranger.[52]

True religion would one day become all but impossible to practice. The Prophet said:

---

[50] *Sahih Bukhari*, n.3650.   [51] *Sahih Bukhari*, n.7068.
[52] *Sahih Muslim*, 'Kitab al-Iman', n.271.

A time will come when persevering in religion will be like grasping a coal.[53]

Superficiality and militant extremism would become widespread. The Prophet also said:

Near the coming of the Hour there will be days during which religious ignorance will spread. [True religious] *Knowledge will vanish, and there will be much of Al-Harj.*[54]

The decline would follow a movement of decline in Christianity and Judaism:

Ye will follow them that were before you span by span and cubit by cubit until if they went down the hole of a poisonous reptile ye would follow them down.[55]

Specifically, the Prophet suggested this movement would first gain ground in the Najd (in fact the birthplace of Wahhabism) and would be characterized by literalism:

There will emerge from the East [of Medina] *a people who will recite the Qur'an but it will not exceed their throats.*[56]

He also said, pointing to the East:

There is sedition there; there is sedition there, from whence will emerge the horn of the devil.[57]

---

[53] *Sunan al-Tirmidhi*, n.2260 (Related by Anas bin Malik and classified as 'good').

[54] *Sahih Bukhari*, n.7063. (*Al-Harj* means 'killing'.)

[55] *Sahih Muslim*, 'Kitab al-Ilm', n.6448.

[56] *Sahih Bukhari*, n.7562. See *also Sahih Muslim*, 'Kitab al-Zakat', n.1064.

[57] *Sahih Bukhari*, n.3279; 'Kitab Bad' al-Khalq', n.11. See also *Sahih Bukhari*, n.3522; 'Kitab al-Manaqib', n.5.

For this reason, finally, the Prophet always refused to bless the Najd. He said:

> *O God! Bless the land of Syria, and bless the land of Yemen. A man [from the Najd] said: O Prophet of God, what about our Najd? The Prophet said: O God! Bless the land of Syria, and bless the land of Yemen. The man [from the Najd] said again: O Prophet of God, what about our Najd? The Prophet said: From there will emerge instability and sedition, and from there will emerge the horn of the devil.*[58]

The Imam Abd al-Rahman al-Akhdari (tenth century) succinctly summarized all these prophecies in the following verses: 'Nothing will remain of the religion of guidance except its name/or of the Qur'an except its script'.[59]

The importance of all these little-known but well-authenticated predictions lies in the fact they forewarn of fundamentalism, situate it, explain it and condemn it. Thus they can be used very effectively to fight it in Muslim eyes and to inoculate against it. They can also evidently be used to alleviate the psychological trauma and confusion of Muslims when faced with people who fight in the name of Islam (or claim to) whilst actually secretly perverting it.

---

[58] *Sahih Bukhari*, n.7094; 'Kitab al-Fitan', n.16. See also *Sahih Bukhari*, n.1037; 'Kitab al-Juma'a', n.27.

[59] '*Lam yabqa min al-din al-huda illa ismuhu / Wa la min al-Qur'ani illa rasmuhu.*' See also fn.25.

POSTSCRIPT

One Year On from September 11th, 2001

THIS STUDY was originally written shortly after September 11th, 2001 for a limited audience. It has, however, been expanded and updated for publication in September 2002. What follows is a brief overview of events over the year between these two dates, in so far as these are relevant to this study.

CHANGE SINCE SEPTEMBER 11TH, 2001

To say the world has changed irrevocably since September 11th, 2001 *because of September 11th, 2001* is axiomatic. Aside from the 'War on Terrorism' (of which more shortly) and the personal tragedies of the 3,000 or so victims of the attacks (and their families and friends), the change encompasses such diverse phenomena as the following: a blow to the US stock market (from which it has yet to recover) and to the world tourist and travel industries; resurgent and indignant American patriotism; *de facto* racial profiling in the West and the return of many Muslims to their countries of origin; the stifling of certain habitual liberties in the USA; and the re-organization of Western administrative (e.g. the proposed 'Department of Homeland Security' in the USA), military, security, intelligence and even financial institutes in order to better combat terrorist threats. More subtly, the attacks on September 11th have, on the one hand, pierced the aura of US invulnerability (if not invincibility, to the USA and the Islamic world alike), and, on the other hand, unfettered (from domestic public opinion and internal politics) the USA as a pro-active and aggressive world superpower, with all the positive and negative consequences this may have for the future. In fact, the full impact of change on the world because of the attacks on September 11th, 2001, cannot fully be assessed for another few years, when current events will have run their course, and history will have given them a context and us a vantage point.

B. 'THE WAR ON TERRORISM'

Successes

Reacting to the terrorist attacks on September 11th, 2001, US President George W. Bush declared 'War on Terrorism' on September 20th, 2001. Since that date this 'war' has been pursued generally very successfully on a number of 'fronts':

(1) On the military front, the USA and its allies have destroyed al-Qa'eda as a significant fighting force, as well as their allies, the Taliban. The USA, or rather the Afghani people, have also 'reclaimed' Afghanistan and have installed there a new, popular and accountable government, thereby depriving al-Qa'eda of the possibility of regrouping. Consequently, there are today few places in the world where military or training camps for Takfiri terrorists are allowed to exist. The USA has (at least by proxy) even pursued its war in places as remote as the Abu Sayyaf's military camps in the jungles of the Philippines.

(2) On the diplomatic and political front, the United States has been equally successful, managing to form and hold together (whether by coercing, cajoling or 'compensating') an international 'grand coalition' against terrorism comprising almost every significant country in the world including foes as bitter as India and Pakistan, and Israel and Syria.

(3) Largely because of the successes on the diplomatic/political front, the third front of the 'War on Terrorism' — the intelligence front — has also fared well. Despite the failure to bring Usama bin Laden and Ayman Zawahiri to justice, there has been fruitful international intelligence co-operation in the 'War on Terrorism': on an almost daily basis over the course of 2002, al-Qa'eda cells, operatives and associates all over the world were exposed and neutralised in countries as far apart as Malaysia and Morocco. Moreover, despite continuing but relatively minor terrorist attacks (by which we mean 'with limited casualties') in countries like Pakistan and India, there have been no terrorist attacks on civilians with casualties in the thousands, or even hundreds — and certainly none in the USA's 'homeland' — between September 11th, 2001 and the present date.

(4) On the financial front, the USA has managed to identify and freeze many of the banks and financial institutes associated with al-Qa'eda (including also some that are perhaps completely innocent) and its associates, and has successfully applied pressure on selected rich Arab individuals and states to cut their indiscriminate funding of Salafi activities.

(5) On the 'containment' front, the successes are partial, but the USA has at least managed to discretely curtail the activities of thousands of Salafi madrasas all over the world from Bosnia to Bangladesh, either by cutting their funding or (as in Pakistan) by inducing the national government to put pressure on them or to make it illegal to teach religious subjects without also teaching the core secular ones (e.g. English, Maths, History, etc.). And although this last strategy might not prove entirely successful (it might simply produce more educated Salafis), it does at least represent a determined effort in the right direction, and does single one out of the primary causes of the spread of both Salafism and 'Takfirism' — the Salafi madrasas.

Postscript

Ongoing Challenges

There are areas, however, where the 'War on Terrorism' has not been so successful. What follows is a brief overview of some of the major ones.

a) **Palestine**

Evidently, the issue of Palestine, which 80 per cent of Muslims consider to be the central grievance against the USA, and which is the one where the 'hearts and minds' of Muslims can most easily be won over, has not been resolved. Despite the USA's unprecedented announcements (first in November 2001 by Secretary of State Colin Powell and then in June 2002 by President Bush himself) of 'US commitment towards a Palestinian State', the issue of Palestine is still nowhere near resolution.

In fact, since September 11th, 2001, the violence between Israelis and Palestinians has only escalated (on both sides) and the death toll has only risen. The trauma of ordinary Israelis living under the terror of random suicide bomb attacks has been more than met tear for tear, and fear for fear, by ordinary Palestinians so that for every Jewish Israeli killed (around 500 from September 2000 to September 2002) there have been at least four Palestinians also killed (around 2,000, depending on the sources, over the same period of time), and for every Israeli wounded there have been at least ten Palestinians also wounded. And the fact remains that the current Palestinian Intifida (uprising) was started in September 28th, 2000 by (then) right-wing leader Ariel Sharon's provocative visit to the sacred *Haram al-Sharif* in Jerusalem, and that since then the entire Palestinian population of approximately three million people has lived intermittently under armed siege, military curfew and economic embargo. Health surveys in August 2002 revealed that one quarter of Palestinian children suffer malnourishment and another quarter suffer severe psychological

trauma from the conflict. This humanitarian situation, whatever the historical and political complexities of the larger conflict, unfortunately ensures that the issue of Palestine will continue to be both a cause and source of terrorism against not
only Israel but the USA as well.

b) Confusion and Conflation vis-à-vis the Concept of 'Terrorism'

One of the singular and surprising omissions of the USA's 'War
on Terrorism' is the lack, to date, of a satisfactory definition of
the term or concept of 'terrorism' (or even 'international terrorism') acceptable to the overwhelming majority of the international community. It may well be asked: 'what has a point of
semantics got to do with a physical war on politically-motivated
murderers?' The answer is: much. For it is impossible to wage
a war — much less win one — without first clearly identifying
who the enemy is. Moreover, with the question of who is a 'terrorist' one must first distinguish them from ordinary murderers
(of which there are 25,000–30,000 every year in the USA
alone), then from ordinary soldiers (who, after all, are professional political killers), and finally between them and 'freedom
fighters'. This last distinction of course is the most problematic
and the one that the USA baulked over, but the fact remains
there is a great *moral difference* between an attack on *military
targets* or armed adult settlers in *militarily occupied territories*
(that are objectively, if not internationally, recognized as such)
and an attack on innocent civilians, women and children in their
home countries. After all, is this not the essential difference
between George Washington and the majority of the Founding
Fathers of the USA and, say, the Oklahoma City Bombers? Did
not the British Colonialists regard the Founding Fathers as terrorists? And could similar arguments not be made about those
who founded Israel, and *a fortiori* the *Gush Emunim*? If 'one

man's food is another man's poison', then certainly also 'one man's freedom-fighter is another man's terrorist'. The only objective moral difference between these lies not in the vindication of history and the retrospective mythology of nation states, but rather in their distinguishing between military and civilian targets for their violence; in the justice of their cause; in their right to self-defence and self-determination, and in the injustice of their oppression. This moral difference, moreover, is one that (as we have shown earlier) is clearly ensconced in traditional Islamic thought, not to mention enshrined in the Geneva Conventions.

As difficult as it may be for Western governments to publicly make this distinction — for fear of encouraging lethal attacks on military targets, and because the subject is inherently too complex to explain easily to the general public in a 'CNN sound-bite' — the failure to clearly identify it in the 'War on Terrorism' has led *de facto* to a number of serious consequences:

(1) It has allowed the USA's agenda (which is essentially a defensive one in view of continuous attacks on the USA culminating in those of September 11th, 2001) to be partly commandeered, not to say hijacked, by other parties and nations. Foremost, amongst these is of course Israel which, with the American media and the pro-Israel lobby supporting it, has largely managed — despite an initial stern rebuff of this idea by the US leadership immediately following September 11th, 2001 — to conflate its situation vis-à-vis the Palestinians with the USA's situation vis-à-vis al-Qa'eda. Now clearly there are many terrorist attacks on Israeli civilians — and these are evidently immoral and unacceptable, to traditional Islam as much as to the West—but not all resistance to Israel can be morally condemned as 'terrorist'. This perhaps is more to the point, just because Israel and the USA both suffer terrorist attacks, it does

not mean that their situations are equivalent: unlike Israel, the USA is not an occupying military power of alien civilian populations and is not out to settle or annex anybody else's territory. Similarly, India has managed to draw a certain parallel with its situation in Kashmir and the USA's 'War on Terror', but again the situation is not entirely equivalent (despite the horrendous terror attacks there) because in historical terms, in the UN's eyes and in the eyes of the majority of Kashmiris themselves, India is an alien occupying power. Thus the lack of a clear definition of the concept of 'terrorism' has allowed countries like Israel and India to present *all* resistance to them as 'terrorism', and allowed them to present themselves as morally equivalent to the US in its war on al-Qaʻeda. This has won them public sympathy in the USA, thereby permitting them to extract valuable concessions from the US government in return for any help in the 'War on Terrorism'.

(2) The lack of a clear definition of the concept of 'terrorism' has multiplied, at least in principle, the USA's enemies to potentially every armed group in the world — ones that target civilians and ones that do not; ones that represent legitimate causes and grievances and ones that do not; and ones that are anti-USA and ones that are not — at a time where the USA needs, *at least first,* to concentrate on its immediate and most dangerous enemies. Evidently also, with the multiplication of international 'enemies' comes the likelihood of less public sympathy for the USA's cause around the world.

(3) The lack of a clear definition of the concept of 'terrorism' has decreased the incentive for armed groups, especially those fighting in the Middle East over the question of Palestine, to make a distinction between military and civilian targets and to avoid the latter, in order to lessen revulsion to them in the United States.

c) Failure to Clearly Identify the Salafi-Takfiris

Despite President Bush's best efforts, following September 11th, 2001, to distinguish between those Muslims who had committed the terrorist attacks against the USA and the 99 per cent of ordinary Muslims who had nothing to do with them and condemn them, and despite his calling Islam 'a religion of peace' and strongly appealing (along with most other American leaders) to Americans not to react with prejudice against ordinary Muslims, there nevertheless occurred in the USA as well as in Europe a rash of 'hate crimes' (including beatings and even murder) against not only Muslims (particularly foreign students), but people who merely looked like Muslims (Indians, Sikhs, etc.). Evidently these ugly reactions were due, in part, to the age-old prejudices, myths, misunderstandings, historical grudges and fears that existed (and still exist) between Muslims and Christians, Arabs and Westerners. They were nevertheless also due, in part, to the lack of a clear terminological distinction in the 'War on Terror' between the different 'types' of Muslims. Admittedly, it is perhaps too much to hope for to expect the Western public to understand the difference between the terms 'traditional Muslim', 'Wahhabi/Salafi' and 'Takfiri' (many Muslims themselves do not understand them and that is precisely part of the problem of terrorism). However, the 'War on Terror' would gain more Islamic popular sympathy if instead of just using terms like 'fundamentalists', 'militants', 'extremists' and 'fanatics' interchangeably and without specificity, the Western official media and Western government leaders, had used more specific and meaningful terms like 'ordinary Muslims' for 'traditional Muslims', 'fundamentalists' for 'Salafis', and 'militant fundamentalists' for 'Takfiris'.[60] Thus, like the failure to

[60] Perhaps the most disingenuous term used for 'Takfiri', however, is 'Islamist'. For example, CNN television presenter Lou Dobbs on his

94

clearly define the concept of 'terrorism', the failure to distinctly
identify different 'Muslim groups' has proved unhelpful in the
'the War on Terrorism': on the one hand, it has left all Muslims
potentially 'branded' in Western eyes, and on the other hand
precisely as a reaction to this indiscriminate 'branding', it has

---

Moneyline show announced, on May 6th, 2002 that he would no longer
use the term 'War on Terror', but henceforth call the war what it really was, a
'War on Islamism', which he then vaguely distinguished from 'moderate
Islam'. Over the next few days dozens of people wrote in to CNN and phoned
to hail Lou Dobbs's 'courage'. However, the idea remains disingenuous for
the following reason: the word 'Islamist' does not formally exist in the English
language and therefore is a 'neologism' or new word, and those who propose
neologisms bear the responsibility for their inherent connotations. Here the
term 'Islamist' to mean cold-blooded terrorists who murder innocent women
and children is misleading because it directly associates these acts with Islam
itself (since this is what the term 'Islamist' immediately recalls), when these
acts are precisely *completely un-Islamic*.

Let us consider for a moment the following inspired sentence from Shakes-
peare's *Macbeth* (uttered by Macbeth himself, in remorse, after he has murdered King Duncan; Act II, Scene II, l.s 61–64): 'Will all great Neptune's
ocean wash this blood / Clean from my hand? No, this my hand will rather /
The multitudinous seas incarnadine / Making the green one red.'

At the time when they were written the words 'multitudinous' and 'incarnadine' were both neologisms, but their connotations were clear because they
took into account their linguistic component parts: 'multitudinous' implied
a 'double multitude', i.e. 'groups of seas', i.e. the seas of the world *and*
those of heaven (alluding to: *And the Spirit of God moved upon the face of the
waters* (Genesis 2)). Similarly, 'incarnadine' recalls not just the red colour
of blood (*carne* obviously being the Latin root for 'flesh', hence 'carnivore'),
but also the idea of dead flesh. Thus a neologism works upon the sounds
and associations of its component parts.

To take another example, if in the light of the revelations in 2002, of
instances of paedophilia that occurred in Catholic churches in the US by
Catholic priests (which were then covered up by officials of the Catholic
Church), someone were to call this phenomenon 'Catholism', the majority
people in the West (certainly most Catholics and linguists) would find this
terminology offensive. Yet this is exactly analogous to calling the September
11th attacks 'Islamism'.

hardened the popular Islamic position. This question can only grow more important if the 'War on Terror' drags on for an extended period of time, and Americans grow weary of their habitual freedoms being curtailed in the name of security without knowing who it is exactly that they are 'at war' with.

We might mention also that part of the blame for this lack of discernment falls squarely on the shoulders of Western academia and 'think tanks'. Despite a veritable industry of books, magazine, articles, editorials, commentaries and studies about the September 11th terrorist attacks in the year since they occurred, few in the West, if any, have specifically diagnosed the 'roots of terror'. The leading books on the subject (books like Gilles Kepel's *Jihad: The Trail of Political Islam*) whilst shrewd and thorough when analysing and documenting the history and politics of the situation, say nothing, however, of the Salafi methods of propagation; completely omit the question of the *doctrinal* differences between the various 'Islamic groups' (perhaps because they *a priori* do not believe in any Islamic doctrines they therefore do not take the question of differences between them seriously); and insist on using the blanket term 'Islamist'. Even what is perhaps the best American book on the subject (certainly one of the most sympathetic to Islam and one of the most respected in the US academic community) Georgetown University Professor John L. Esposito's *Unholy War: Terror in the Name of Islam* ignores the basic hermeneutical differences as regards the interpretation of the Qur'an and the *Hadith* that separate between traditional Muslims, Salafis and Takfiris.[61]

---

[61] All Esposito says about Salafi hermeneutics is the following: 'The Wahhabi religious vision or brand of Islam, named after Muhammad bin Abd al-Wahhab, has been a staple of the Saudi government, a source of their religious and political legitimation. It is a strict, puritanical faith that emphasizes literal interpretation of the Qur'an and the *Sunnah* (example) of the

d) The US-Saudi Political Roller-Coaster, September 2001–September 2002

The US-Saudi diplomatic relationship, dating back essentially to SOCAL's initial oil concession in May 1933, almost seventy years ago, is one of the most important in the world. It the relationship between the largest importer in the world (the USA) and the largest exporter in the world (Saudi Arabia) of the most important commodity in the world (oil — water is not usually considered a commodity), it is also the relationship between the world's only superpower and the Arab's world's premier power.[62] It is a relationship that has seen five Saudi kings and over a dozen US presidents. It a relationship that has survived over fifty years of Arab-Israeli conflict, the 1973 Oil Embargo, and Saudi King Faisal's assassination in 1975. It is a relationship that held fast during the Second World War, became a covert alliance during the Cold War, and became an open partnership during the 1991 Gulf War. Finally, it is a relationship of great mutual benefit. The unspoken axioms of the relationship are that the Saudis (1) sell the USA oil at slightly under market prices; (2) the Saudis use their influence in OPEC and their massive output capacity to keep world oil prices down; and (3) the Saudis 'recycle' US 'petrodollars' back into the US economy as much as possible by buying US products (especially arms)

Prophet Muhammad and the absolute oneness of God' (John L. Esposito, *Unholy War: Terror in the Name of Islam*, Oxford UP, 2002, p.6) And: '*Wahhabi* describes Saudi Arabia's ultraconservative, puritanical brand of Islam: literalist, rigid, and exclusivist ... the Wahhabis seek to impose their strict beliefs and interpretations, which are not commonly shared by other Sunni or by Shii Muslims throughout the Muslim world' (ibid., p.106).

[62] 'Premier' because although not the geographically largest (Sudan, closely followed by Algeria) nor the most populous (Egypt), nevertheless the one with the highest GDP and the one which contains the holy cities of Mecca and Medina.

and by investing in the USA. The Americans, for their part, (1) protect Saudi Arabia and guarantee their security (witness the 1991 Gulf War); (2) agree not to bring up the issue of democracy in the kingdom; and (3) do not expose the issue of corruption in the kingdom ($50 billion of which was admitted to, astonishingly, by Saudi ambassador to the USA, Prince Bandar bin Sultan, on a PBS *Frontline* show on October 9th, 2001). Both sides also agree to openly disagree about Israel.

Since September 11th, 2001, however, the US-Saudi relationship has suffered a period of crisis not seen since the 1973 Oil Embargo. The immediate seeds for the crisis were laid down by the fact that Usama bin Laden was born a Saudi citizen and that fifteen out of the nineteen September 11th hijackers were also Saudis. By the end of October, 2001 there was beginning to emerge, from the USA, official or 'semi-official' public criticism of Saudi Arabia. Influential US Republican Senator John McCain declared on October 28th, 2001, on CNN's *Late Edition* that the Saudi monarchy was not doing 'what the president asked all countries to do, and that is to take sides' in the War on Terrorism. By the end of December 2001, there was a rash of articles and editorials in almost every major US newspaper criticizing the Saudis. In response the Saudi leadership, was making fiery and defiant speeches at home. By the February 2002, the Saudis, having finally realized the gravity of the situation, and being shocked by the ferocity of some of the criticism, had engineered a three-pronged strategy to diffuse the problem: (1) they quite simply increased and sped up covert cooperation with the US, acquiescing to many of their demands.[63] (2) They initiated a massive public relations campaign in the

[63] Evidence of this can perhaps be seen in the statements of Salafi Sheikhs like Ibn 'Uthaymin making, for the first time, conciliatory statements towards traditional Muslims, including Sufis. Significantly also, after an

US to improve their image.[64] (3) They floated a comprehensive Arab-Israeli Peace Plan,[65] which was finally unanimously adopted by the Arab League Summit in Beirut on March 28th, 2002, offering Israel for the first time *explicitly* full peace and normal relations *with the entire Arab World* in return for, basically, Israel's withdrawal from all occupied territories and the establishment of a Palestinian sovereign state. This 'rehabilitation plan' at first seemed to have the desired effect, for by April 2002 the tone of the US press about Saudi Arabia had improved[66] and on April 25th, 2002, Saudi Crown Prince

---

incident where at least fifteen girls died in the Hijaz province of Saudi Arabia because their Wahhabi teachers would not let them out of their school because they were improperly dressed *even though the school was on fire,* Crown Prince Abdullah bin Abd al-Aziz, transferred administrative control of girls' public schools from the religious authorities to the more modern and moderate Ministry of Education.

[64] The Saudis spent millions on a public relations campaign handled inside the USA by companies like Qorvis Communications. They ran advertisements with slogans like 'Keep your eyes, ears and minds open!' and 'The People of Saudi Arabia: Allies against Terrorism' in a number of major US cities. They also encouraged many Saudi graduates of US universities, including women, to return to their *Alma Mater*s and give talks to students and teachers promoting their country.

[65] The plan was initially 'leaked' on February 8th, 2002 by journalist Thomas Friedman in *The New York Times*, reporting that he had seen a copy of the plan in Crown Prince Abdullah bin Abd al-Aziz's desk. The plan initially made no mention of the key issue of 'the Right to Return' for Palestinian refugees, and seemed to make historic concessions on Palestinian territories in Jerusalem (the Crown Prince's ubiquitous advisor Adel al-Jubair was reported in the US media as saying: 'We are not in the real estate business'), but by the time the plan was adopted by the Arab Summit in March both the Palestinian 'Right to Return' and the 'Return to pre-1967 borders in Jerusalem' were reaffirmed.

[66] For example, *Newsweek* in April 2002 featured articles hailing 'The once and future kings of oil', asking 'are the Saudis invincible?' and pointing out how the Saudis had always worked to moderate the price of oil.

Abdullah bin Abd al-Aziz was invited to President Bush's private ranch near Crawford, Texas (he was only the third world leader to be invited there after Prime Minister Blair and President Putin). This proved only a temporary respite, however, for by August 2002 a series of events had raised tensions again. First, Senators Arlen Specter R-Pennsylvania and Joseph Lieberman D-Connecticut accused Saudi Arabia of supporting Hamas and terrorism. Second, the US media leaked reports of a presentation given to a Pentagon board of advisors by the RAND Corporation, describing Saudi Arabia as an 'enemy' and advocating the seizure by US troops of the Saudi oil fields (shortly after this Defence Secretary Rumsfeld phoned his Saudi counterpart Prince Sultan bin Abd al-Aziz to decry the report, and distance US policy from it. Third, a group of families of '9/11' victims raised a multi-trillion dollar court-case against Sudan and some senior Saudi princes (including the powerful Prince Sultan himself) for their 'role' in supporting Usama bin Laden. By way of reaction, Saudi newspapers in Riyadh called not only for a review of the US-Saudi strategic relationship and of Saudi investments in the US, but also for a counter court-case against the US for their own connections to Usama bin Laden during the Afghan War (1979–1989). Now obviously one can over-interpret all these events, but clearly the US-Saudi relationship was once again suffering tensions.

Thus for the year following September 11th, 2001, unprecedented strains appeared in the US-Saudi relationship, with some in the US laying part of the blame for the terrorist attacks on Saudi Arabia (and with others perhaps seeing an opportunity to settle old scores and diminish Saudi influence in Washington DC). However, from the point of view of the US's 'War of Terror', the following must be borne in mind as regards Saudi Arabia:

(1) To blame solely the Saudis for the world-wide spreading of Salafism, and consequently 'Takfirism', is to ignore or to be ignorant of the US's own role in this 'spreading' especially during its most aggressive phase in the 1980s.

(2) To identify the Saudi Royal Family wholesale with Salafism is, as we have tried to point out, not strictly accurate, despite their historical origins and political links. Nor is it accurate to identify Salafism wholesale with 'Takfirism'.

(3) The Saudis may have reasons of their own to want to bring Salafism more in line with traditional Islam, not the least of which is the growing power and independence of Salafi preachers inside Saudi Arabia itself. Also the Saudis understand full well that the world around them is changing and that at some point change is inevitable even in Saudi Arabia itself. They know that if they do not take the lead in this change and direct its course themselves, they may well be its first casualties. This situation is exacerbated by the fact that the country's top princes (arguably Crown Prince Abdullah bin Abd al-Aziz; Prince Sultan bin Abd al-Aziz, the Minister of Defence; Prince Naif bin Abd al-Aziz, the Minister of Interior; and Prince Salman bin Abd al-Aziz, the Governor of Riyadh) are all in their seventies so that over the next ten to fifteen years the country will likely have a succession of very short reigns whose brevity is bound to cause upheaval and instability.

(4) The only people capable of quietly and seamlessly checking and moderating Salafism are the Saudis themselves, not only because they sit atop of the hierarchy of many of the institutes that propagate Salafism, but because they have the best knowledge of them and the longest experience with them. Of course, in replacing Salafi preachers abroad the Saudis will undoubtedly need the help of countries like Egypt and Morocco, who have strong traditional Islamic establishments and cadres of moderate

and learned preachers ready to fill the Salafis' shoes, but the Saudis' situation is currently helped by the personal credibility, all over the Islamic world, enjoyed by the *de facto* ruler of Saudi Arabia, Crown Prince Abdullah bin Abd al-Aziz.

(5) The Saudi population itself is in general quite staunchly Salafi — far more so than the Royal Family, a small minority of Westernized liberals and Shi'a notwithstanding. Clandestine reports show that at least 80 per cent of Saudis either sympathize with Usama bin Laden or do not believe he was responsible for the terror attacks on the USA.[8] Moreover, the only people who are at all politically organized in Saudi Arabia outside of the state's apparatus are the Salafi preachers, so that the only likely alternative to the Saudi Royal Family is hard-core Salafism, possibly even Takfirism. The alternative in Saudi Arabia is not between the Saudi royals and an Arab JFK, but between the Saudi royals and a Salafi Khomeini!

(6) The Saudis *have been* co-operating with the 'War on Terror', but have their own difficult internal pressures to contend with, not the least being those generated by Takfiris themselves. The Saudis cannot move too quickly without fear of a backlash from their own hard-core Salafi population.

(7) The embarrassment and undermining of the Saudi regime — its being caught between the West and popular opinion in Saudi Arabia — has always been Usama bin Laden's ultimate strategic objective, not merely in the September 11th, 2001, but in all his attacks on US targets over the years. These attacks are thus merely the means to an end, which is, first, a Takfiri state in Saudi Arabia, and, then, a united Takfiri Islamic world (under Usama bin Laden or someone like him). Undermining

---

[67] This is particularly true of the central provinces, but not necessarily so for the Eastern and Western regions where a considerable proportion of Saudis are not Salafis.

the Saudis means rewarding Usama bin Laden and bringing his dreams closer to realization.

(8) Scenarios that call for the US to invade the Saudi oil fields are extremely dangerous, not to say irrational: they would cause untold instability, shift international politics and the global balance of power in unforeseeable and explosive ways, destabilize the world's economic system and potentially create a 'terrorist' out of every Muslim in the world. They constitute the exact opposite of all of the stated aims and ideals of the 'War on Terror'.

In summary, we can say that Saudi support is crucial for the 'War on Terrorism', to check and moderate Salafism and to eradicate 'Takfirism'. In order for the Saudis to grant it they will expect support and encouragement, not attacks and accusations, which on the contrary may 'harden' their position. Thus there is no alternative to the Saudis. To fight terror, all roads lead to Riyadh.

C. CONCLUSION

In conclusion then we note that during the year following the September 11th, 2001 terrorist attacks on the USA, President Bush's 'War on Terror' has proceeded successfully on the military, intelligence, diplomatic/political and financial fronts. However, the root causes of terror are still present in the Islamic world. In order to tackle these more subtle and sophisticated strategies are called for. Specifically, what is needed is: (1) a clearer definition and understanding of precisely who the enemy is and who he is not, (and thus a more precise understanding of the Islamic world in general); (2) The resolution of factors that give rise to an atmosphere in the Islamic world where terror can take root and find popular support, and in particular the resolution of the ongoing problem of Palestine; (3) A holistic strategy to contain the spread of Salafism, 'reeling back' the Salafis into Traditional Islam, and thereby depriving 'Takfirism' of its initial breeding ground.

If the USA does not do this, and deals only with the concrete manifestations of terrorist networks and infrastructures, the problem will have been postponed and not solved. Then it is only a matter of time before terrorism raises its head again, this time on a more devastating scale, for the terrorists will have learned from their mistakes and failures. And in a world such as ours — a world where nuclear bombs are missing from the ex-Soviet arsenal and where viruses to decimate humanity are created daily in laboratories — this absolutely must not be permitted to happen.

FURTHER READING
IN ENGLISH

Muhammad Asad, *The Road to Mecca,* Dar al-Andalus, Gibraltar, 1980.

Eleanor Abdella Doumato, 'The Ambiguity of Sharia and the Politics of 'Rights' in Saudi Arabia', in Mahnaz Afkhami (ed), *Faith and Freedom: Women's Rights in the Muslim World,* I.B. Tauris, London, 1995.

Gai Eaton, *Islam and the Destiny of Man,* Islamic Texts Society, Cambridge, 1994 [1985].

Kerim Fenari, 'Hadiths of Najd and Tamim', article available at www. masud. co.uk

G. Finati, *Narrative of the Life and Adventures of Giovanni Finati,* London, 1830.

John S. Habib, *Ibn Saud's Warriors of Islam: The Ikhwan of Najd and their role in the creation of the Saudi Kingdom,* New York University Press, New York, 1998.

Fred Halliday, *Two Hours that Shook the World. September, 11, 2001: Causes and Consequences,* Saqi Books, London, 2002.

David Holden and Richard Johns, *The House of Saud,* Pan Books, London, 1982.

Nuh Ha Mim Keller, *Al-Maqasid: Nawawi's Manual of Islam,* Amana Publications, Beltsville, 2002 [2nd ed.].

Gilles Kepel, *Jihad: The Trail of Political Islam,* I.B. Tauris, London, 2002.

Further Reading

Martin Lings, *Muhammad: His life based on the earliest sources,* Islamic Texts Society, Cambridge, 1995.

Sayf ad-Din Ahmad Ibn Muhammad, *Al-Albani Unveiled: An Exposition of His Errors and Other Important Issues,* Islamic Promotions, Blackburn, England, 1994.

Abdal Hakim Murad, 'The Problem of Anti-Madhhabism', *Islamica,* 2:2, March 1998, pp.31–39.

——'Islamic Spirituality: The Revolution Within', *Islamica,* 1:3, August 1993, pp.5–9.

Sachiko Murata and William C. Chittick, *The Vision of Islam,* Paragon House, Minnesota, 2001.

Seyyed Hossein Nasr, *The Heart of Islam,* HarperSanFrancisco, San Francisco, 2002.

——*Ideals and Realities of Islam,* HarperCollins, London, 1994.

Ahmed Rashid, *Taliban: Islam, Oil and the New Great Game in Central Asia,* I. B. Tauris, London, 2002 [2nd ed.].

Ameen Rihani, *Ibn Sa'oud of Arabia: His People and His Land,* Constable and Co Ltd., London, 1928.

Alexei Vassiliev, *A History of Saudi Arabia,* New York University Press, New York, 1998.

Jamal Effendi al-'Iraqi al-Sidqi al-Zahawi, *The Doctrine of Ahl al-Sunna versus the 'Salafi' Movement,* (translated and edited by Shaykh Muhammad Hisham Kabbani), As-Sunna Foundation of America, California, 1996.

INDEX

Aal al-Sheikh, 'Abd al-Rahman, 56
Aal al-Sheikh, 'Abd al-'Aziz, 33
Abd al-Hamid II, 13n
'Abduh, Muhammad, 20n
Abdullah bin Abd al-Aziz, 100
Abraham, 52
abrogation, 25–26
absolute *ijtihad,* 23
Abu Bakr, xii, 46
Abu Sayyaf, 67, 73, 88
activism, 55
al-Afghani, Jamal al-Din, 20n
Afghanistan, 19–20
Aga Khans, 11
Ahmadiyya, 12
Ajyad, Salafi destruction of, 40
al-Akhdari, Abd al-Rahman, 86
Alawis, 12
al-Albani, Nasr al-Din, 28
Albania, xi
Algeria, 9, 46, 71
allegorical verses of the
    Qur'an, 31
analogy. *See Qiyas,* 29
anthropomorphism, 31–32
al-Aqsa Mosque, 82
Arab League Summit, 99
Arab nationalism, 18
Arabic language, 24–26
Arab-Israeli Peace Plan, 99
Arab-Israeli War, 18
Arnaouti, Abd al-Qadir, 28
Arnaouti, Shu'ayb, 28

art, Salafi rejection of, 35–36
al-Assad, Hafez, 53n
Asbab al-Nuzul, 25
'Asqalani, 6
assassination, 48
Ataturk, Kamal, 14
Azhar, 13n
Azraqi, 6

Babis, 12
Badawiyya, 11
Baghawi, 6
Bahais, 12
Bamiyan, 39
Bandar bin Sultan, 98
al-Banna, Hasan, 15n
Baqi', Salafi destruction of, 40
Bashir, Omar, 16
Bayhaqi, 6
Baydawi, 5
bin 'Abd Al-Wahhab,
    Muhammad, 17, 23, 34, 57
bin Baz, 'Abd al-'Aziz, 31, 56
bin Laden, Usama
    1998 Fatwa, 68, 80–83
    bombing of USS Cole, xi
    formative military training,
        19–20
bin Sa'ud, 'Abd al-'Aziz, 18, 40, 59
book publishing, Salafi, 61–62
Bosnia, genocide in, 9
Britain, xi
Bukhari, 5

Index

Index

Holland, xi
Holy Law, rejection of principles of, 22–23
Huntington, Samuel, 8n
Hutus, ix–xn

Ibadis, 10
Ibn Hanbal, Ahmad, 5, 29
Ibn Ishaq, 6
Ibn Kathir, 5
Ibn Maja, 6
Ibn Qudama, 82
Ibn Sa'd, 6
Ibn Sa'ud, Muhammad, 18, 57n
Ibn Taymiyya, Ahmad, 17, 82
  literalism, 32
  rejection of consensus, 30
Ibn 'Uthaymin, 98n
Idarat Hayat al-Buhuth wal Da'wa wal-Irshad, 55–56
al-Ighata al-Islamiyya al-'Alamiyya, 64
Ihsan, 2–4
Ihya' 'Ulum al-Din, 6
ijma', 22n, 30
ijtihad
  closing 'doors' of, 23n
  absolute, 23–24n
Ikhwan Muslimin. *See* Muslim Brotherhood
illiteracy, 50
Iman, 2–4
India, xi, 9, 93
Indonesia, 61, 67
Interahamwe gangs, ix–xn
internet, 65–66
Iranian Revolution, 17
Irfan, 11
Isaac, 52
Islam

compared with Christianity, 7–8
decline of, 84
fundamentalism, 12, 14–17
history, 1–2, 6–7
modernism, 12–14
mysticism, 11
orthodoxy, 10–12
principles of, 2–4
sacred texts, 5–6
Islamic Development Bank, 19
Islamic Jihad, 73
Islamic world
  bewildered by the 20th century, 51
  economic problems, 9
  education, 49–50
  humiliation, 50–51
  population distribution, 7
  warfare, 9–10
  weaknesses of, 8–10
Isma'ilis, 11n
Israel, xi, 51–53
'Israiliyat, 26
Italy, xi

Ja'faris, 11
Jalalayn, 5
Jahiliyya poetry, 6, 24
Jama'at-ul-Tabligh, 70n
Jama'at-i-Islami, 15n
Jam'iyat Ihya al-Turath, 55
al-Jazairi, Abd al-Qadir, 63n
al-Jazuli, Imam, 6
Jebusites, 52
Jeddah, Salafi destruction of, 40
Jerusalem, 52
Jews, 51–53
Jihad
  rules of, 45–46

Index

Index

Index

Salafism
  absolute *ijtihad,* 23
  anthropomorphism, 31–32
  destruction of sacred sites,
    39–41
  disrespect of the Prophet,
    32–34
  hatred of the United States, xi
  Ibn Sa'ud, Muhammad, 18
  influence on Muslim
    Brotherhood, 16
  introduced, 15
  literalism, 30–31
  media control, 61–62
  organizational structure, 54–59
  rejection of consensus, 30
  rejection of philosophy, 34
  rejection of *Qiyas,* 29
  rejection of Qur'anic exegesis,
    26–28
  rejection of sacred art, 35–36
  rejection of science of
    language, 24–26
  rejection of theology, 34
  rejection of transmitted
    knowledge, 21
  revisions of *Hadith,* 28–29
  rise of, 17–20
  Saudi Royal Family and, 57–58
  women's rights, 36–37
Salafi-Takfiris. *See* Takfiris
salaried sheikhs, 59
Salman bin Abd al-Aziz, 101
Saudi Arabia, 18
  alliance with Pakistan and
    USA, 19
  Arab-Israeli Peace Plan, 99
  Najd, 25
  relationship with USA, 97–103
  Royal Family, 56–59

support for Usama bin Laden,
  100–102
schools, 19, 60
September 11th, shock of, ix–x
  affects of, 87–88
Serbia, xi
Shadhiliyya, 11
al-Shafi'i, Imam, 6
Shafi'i school, 10
Shah Massoud, Ahmed, 47, 63n,
  75–76n
Shamil Daghestani, 63n
Shari'a. See Holy Law
Sharon, Ariel, 90
Shaykhis, 12
Shawkani, 5
Shi'a Islam, 10–12
  historical lies against, 63
  revolutionary Shi'ism, 15, 17
al-Sijistani, 5
smoking, 43
Somalia, xi
Spain, 6–7
Specter, Arlen, 100
Standard Oil of California, 18
stock market, 87
Sudan, 97n
Sufism, 11
  historical lies against, 62
  Salafi rejection of, 33–34, 35
Suhayli, 6
Suhrawardiyya, 11
suicide, 47–48
Sultan bin Abd al-Aziz, 100–1
Sunni Islam, 10–12

Tabari, 6, 26
Tabligh movement, 70
tafsir. See exegesis
Taha, Abu Yasir Rifa'i Ahmad, 80

Index

al-Tahhan, Abd al-Rahim, 27
Tahriri (Liberation) Party, 15n
Takfiris
  assassination, 48
  combating, 79
  identifying, 94-97
  organizational structures, 72–74
  rejection of political authority,
    43–44
  rise of, 19
  suicide, 47–48
  understanding of *Jihad,* 46–47
tawassul, 42
technology in the Islamic world, 8
temporary marriage, 39, 66
terrorism
  lack of clear definition of, 91
  war on, 88–89
  terrorist cells, 72–73
theology, Salafi rejection of, 34
thuggery, 65
Tijaniyya, 11
tourist industry, 87
traditional Islam, 12
transmitted knowledge, 21
travelling Salafi army, 73–74
Turabi, Hasan, 16
Tutsis, ix–xn
Twin Towers, ix–x

'Umar ibn al-Khattab, 2, 45,
United Nations Security
  Council, 9
United States of America
  hatred of, xi

hijacked by other nations, 92
killing Americans, 82
patriotism, 87
role in Israeli-Palestinian
  conflict, 51–53
universities, 60
USS *Cole,* xi
Usul al-fiqh, 22–23

Vilayet i-Faqih, 17

wahhabism. *See* Salafism
al-Wahidi, 5
Waqidi, 6
War on Terrorism, 88–89
warfare, 9–10
Western-style education, 49–50
women's rights, 36–37

Yashrutiyya, 11
Yemen
  USS *Cole,* bombing of, xi
  Zeidis, 11
Young Turks, 13n

Zakat, 60
Zamakhshari, 5
Zanzibar, xi
Zawahiri, Ayman, 73, 80
Zawaj Misyar marriage, 38
Zawaj Mu'aqqat marriage, 39,
  66
Zawaj Sirri marriage, 38
Zeidis, 11
Zogby polls, 51n

113

ABOUT THE AUTHOR

Professor Vincenzo Oliveti is considered one of Europe's leading experts on the Arabic language and on Islamic Studies. His books have been translated into six languages.